POLITICS 101

Politics 101

**SANDEEP
CHAVAN**

GYRUS VISION

Disclaimer

This book is intended to provide a general overview of various political, economic, and social issues in India. The views, interpretations, and opinions expressed within are those of the author and do not necessarily represent the views of any government, political party, organization, or institution. The content is based on publicly available information, research, and the author's understanding at the time of writing.

The book should not be construed as professional legal, political, or economic advice. Readers are encouraged to conduct their own research or seek professional guidance for specific questions or issues they may encounter. While every effort has been made to ensure the accuracy of the information, the author does not take responsibility for any errors or omissions.

All historical and current events discussed are interpreted through a personal lens and should be seen as part of a broader discussion about India's socio-political landscape. The inclusion of specific laws, policies, or reforms does not imply endorsement or criticism, but rather serves to inform readers about the complexities and nuances of governance and public affairs in India.

This book is for educational and informational purposes only. The author disclaims liability for any losses or damages, whether direct or indirect, resulting from the use or interpretation of the material contained within this book.

Preface

Politics 101: What They Don't Teach You in School is an attempt to bridge the gap between formal education and the practical realities of how politics shapes the world we live in. As citizens of the world's largest democracy, it is essential to understand not just the structure of governance but also the underlying dynamics of power, influence, and decision-making that impact our everyday lives.

In today's rapidly evolving political landscape, it is more important than ever for young people to be informed and engaged. Yet, many of us find that the basics of politics are often shrouded in jargon or left out of our formal education. This book aims to provide a clear, accessible introduction to Indian politics, explain its complexities, and highlight the opportunities and challenges it presents for the next generation of leaders and citizens.

The journey of writing this book stemmed from a desire to offer readers a practical understanding of politics—one that goes beyond textbook definitions and touches on real-world issues like corruption, electoral reform, economic policies, and youth engagement. The intent is not only to inform but also to inspire, encouraging readers to participate actively in the political process, whether by voting, campaigning, or even running for office.

Each chapter in this book explores different facets of Indian politics, from the roots of corruption to the future of digital campaigning, and emphasizes the role of young people in shaping the future. This book is written for students, educators, professionals, and anyone who wants to better understand how political power operates and how they can influence change within the system.

In writing **Politics 101**, I hope to demystify the subject of politics and make it approachable for everyone, because ultimately, politics is not just about leaders and policies—it is about us. It is about the choices we make, the voices we raise, and the future we build together.

Let this book serve as a guide to understanding the power of politics and a call to action for those who wish to create meaningful change.

— *Er. Sandeep Chavan*
Educator, Engineer, and Political Enthusiast

CONTENTS

| 1 |

Introduction

Setting the Stage

Politics is not just something that happens far away in government offices or during election season; it's a force that shapes nearly every aspect of our lives. From the schools we attend to the roads we drive on, politics decides the quality of our education, the healthcare we receive, and even the opportunities we have to succeed in life. Yet, for many young people, politics often feels distant, complicated, and irrelevant. It's a subject that is rarely discussed in-depth in school, leaving most of us with a vague understanding of its true impact.

In fact, politics is often seen as something negative—a messy arena filled with corruption, scandals, and broken promises. The word itself may evoke feelings of frustration or disinterest. Many young people shy away from politics, believing that their individual involvement won't make a difference, or worse, they think they're too young to understand how it works. But the truth is, **politics isn't just for politicians**—it's for all of us.

In this book, we'll break down the complex world of politics into simple, understandable terms. We'll help you see how political decisions made in New Delhi or your local state capitals affect your everyday life. More importantly, we'll show you how understanding these processes give you the power to shape them. **If you want to see change—whether in education, job creation, or environmen-**

tal policies—you must first understand how political systems work.

By the time you finish this book, you'll understand why politics is something you should care about. You'll learn how it affects the choices you make and the life you lead. You'll also see that ignoring politics doesn't make you immune to its impact. **The more you understand, the more empowered you'll be to make changes, whether in your local community or at a national level**.

This isn't just a lesson in civics; it's a guide to becoming an active participant in shaping your future. Politics may often be kept in the background of mainstream education, but in reality, **it's the background of everything we do**. The sooner you understand it, the more prepared you'll be to navigate life's challenges with clarity, confidence, and influence.

Politics in Everyday Life

Imagine waking up in the morning. You grab your mobile phone, check your social media feeds, and find a mix of entertainment, advertisements, and news. Even in those first few moments of your day, politics is already at play. The price of your internet plan, the regulations surrounding digital privacy, and even what content you're exposed to can be traced back to political decisions. And that's just the start.

Let's break down some examples of how **politics infiltrates everyday life**:

- **Jobs**: Whether or not there are enough good jobs in your city isn't just a result of market forces. Government policies on employment, taxation, and trade agreements play a massive role in shaping industries. For instance, political decisions about the promotion of local industries or foreign investments can directly influence which companies flourish and which collapse.

When governments promise job creation, they are making political decisions that will affect thousands of lives.

- **Education**: The school or college you attend, the syllabus you follow, the teachers who instruct you—all of these are influenced by political decisions. Government funding for public schools, the availability of scholarships, and even the subjects offered in universities are all the result of policies created by politicians. For instance, the New Education Policy (NEP) 2020 in India seeks to reform the entire education system, which directly impacts millions of students.

- **Infrastructure**: The roads you take to get to school or work, the bridges that connect your city, and even the electricity that powers your home—these are all products of political action. Infrastructure development is often touted as a political achievement, and the funds allocated for these projects are determined by government budgets. A lack of political will can lead to delays in necessary infrastructure, which in turn affects everyday life.

- **Healthcare**: The cost of healthcare, the availability of hospitals, the prices of medicines, and even public health campaigns are shaped by political decisions. Government policies decide how much is spent on healthcare, what kind of treatments are subsidized, and which diseases get attention. For instance, during the COVID-19 pandemic, the way governments handled the crisis—from lockdowns to vaccination programs—was a matter of political decision-making.

- **Entertainment and Media**: Even the films and TV shows you watch can be influenced by politics. Government censorship, the regulation of the entertainment industry, and the financial incentives for content creators are all part of political frameworks. Additionally, the news media, often labeled the "fourth pillar of democracy," is heavily influenced by politics. News outlets often reflect political biases, and understanding these biases is crucial for making informed decisions about the world around you.

The message is simple: **politics is everywhere**. It touches every corner of life, from the most personal moments to the broadest social trends. That's why it's essential for young people to grasp the importance of political decisions. Whether you realize it or not, your future is being shaped by politics right now.

Instead of being passive observers, you can take control of your own destiny by understanding how these decisions are made and who makes them. This book is your guide to unlocking that knowledge.

With this newfound understanding, you'll no longer view politics as something that happens "out there" or something irrelevant to your life. You'll see it as a powerful tool that can be used to create positive change—both for yourself and for the larger society. If you want better jobs, a cleaner environment, or more accessible education, understanding politics is your first step in making those dreams a reality.

In the chapters ahead, we'll dive deep into the hidden truths of how politics shapes our world, exploring both the positive potential and the negative consequences of the political process. We'll talk about corruption, power struggles, and the game of influence. But most importantly, we'll show you how, armed with knowledge, **you can become a force for change**.

Welcome to **Politics 101**—the class that no school will ever teach you but is essential for your future.

| 2 |

What is Politics?

Definitions and Origins of Politics

What is Politics? Politics is one of the most ancient and fundamental aspects of human society, and its influence extends to every sphere of life. It governs how societies are structured, how laws are made and enforced, and how power and resources are distributed among people. To fully understand politics, we must first explore its various definitions and trace its origins to better appreciate its evolving nature in human history.

Definitions of Politics

Politics can be defined in numerous ways, depending on the context in which it is being discussed. At its core, politics is about **power**—who has it, how they use it, and how they maintain or challenge it. Here are several definitions that capture different dimensions of politics:

1. **Politics as Governance**: In its most basic sense, politics refers to the process of governance. This includes the mechanisms through which societies create rules and laws, enforce them, and resolve disputes. According to this view, politics is about managing the affairs of a society, ensuring that order is maintained, and justice is delivered. Political institutions like governments, courts, and parliaments are central to this definition.

2. **Politics as Conflict Resolution**: Politics is often seen as a way of managing conflict. Human societies are made up of individuals and groups with different interests, goals, and values. Politics provides a framework through which these differences can be negotiated and conflicts resolved. This perspective sees politics as the art of compromise, where various stakeholders come together to find common ground or make decisions that balance competing interests.

3. **Politics as Power Dynamics**: A more critical definition views politics as the struggle for power and influence. In any society, certain individuals or groups hold more power than others. Politics is the process through which these power relationships are established, contested, and sometimes overturned. This definition emphasizes the role of power, authority, and control in shaping political outcomes and societal structures.

4. **Politics as Public Decision-Making**: Another approach to defining politics focuses on its role in public decision-making. Politics is about making decisions that affect the public, such as setting economic policies, deciding on social programs, and determining foreign policy. Political leaders are chosen to represent the will of the people, but their decisions must also balance the broader public interest with the needs of specific constituencies.

5. **Politics as Ideology and Identity**: In contemporary times, politics is often closely tied to ideologies (like liberalism, socialism, conservatism) and group identities (such as caste, religion, ethnicity, gender). Political movements often arise from deeply held beliefs about how society should be organized or from marginalized groups seeking greater representation or rights. Identity politics, where groups mobilize based on shared identities, has become a dominant force in global and Indian politics.

Origins of Politics: A Historical Perspective

The origins of politics can be traced back to the very foundations of human civilization. As early human societies evolved from hunter-gatherer groups to more complex agrarian communities, the need for organized leadership, laws, and decision-making became apparent. This gave rise to early forms of governance, social hierarchies, and power structures.

1. **Primitive Societies and Tribal Leadership**: In pre-civilizational societies, leadership was often based on kinship and tribal affiliations. Elders or tribal leaders would make decisions for the group, often based on traditions or collective wisdom. The primary goal was survival, and political decisions revolved around resource allocation, defense, and conflict resolution within and between tribes.

2. **City-States and the Birth of Political Thought**: As human societies settled into agricultural communities, they grew into city-states, particularly in ancient civilizations like Mesopotamia, Egypt, and Greece. These early political structures gave rise to more formalized systems of government, often ruled by monarchs, priests, or councils. In ancient Greece, particularly in Athens, we see the birth of political philosophy, where thinkers like **Plato** and **Aristotle** began to theorize about the nature of governance, justice, and democracy. They asked fundamental questions that continue to shape political thought: *Who should rule? What makes a government legitimate? What is the role of the citizen in politics?*

3. **Monarchies and Empires**: As political systems evolved, we witnessed the rise of monarchies and empires across the world, from ancient Rome to the Maurya and Gupta empires in India, to the Ming dynasty in China. Politics in this era was heavily concentrated in the hands of emperors, kings, and queens, whose rule was often justified by divine right or military conquest. Political power was centralized, and governance often fo-

cused on expanding territory, maintaining internal order, and managing the bureaucracy that governed large populations.

4. **The Enlightenment and Modern Democracy**: The modern political landscape was profoundly shaped by the **Enlightenment** period in Europe during the 17th and 18th centuries. Thinkers like **John Locke**, **Jean-Jacques Rousseau**, and **Montesquieu** questioned the legitimacy of absolute monarchies and proposed ideas of individual rights, separation of powers, and representative democracy. The **American Revolution** (1775-1783) and the **French Revolution** (1789) were key moments in the transition from monarchy to democratic governance. These revolutions introduced the concepts of political equality, the rule of law, and the protection of individual freedoms—principles that are now embedded in many of today's democratic constitutions, including India's.

5. **Colonialism and Post-Colonial Politics**: The political history of the modern world cannot be understood without acknowledging the era of colonialism. European powers, driven by economic motives and the ideology of imperialism, colonized large parts of Africa, Asia, and the Americas. In India, British colonial rule profoundly shaped the political landscape, leading to the rise of nationalist movements and the eventual push for independence. The **Indian National Congress (INC)**, founded in 1885, became a pivotal force in mobilizing Indians against British rule and advocating for self-governance, which culminated in India's independence in 1947.

6. **Post-Independence Politics and Nation-Building**: In post-colonial India, the process of nation-building brought forth the challenge of uniting a diverse and divided population. The framing of the **Indian Constitution** laid the foundation for democratic governance, with universal suffrage, federalism, and protection of fundamental rights. The early political leadership, under figures like **Jawaharlal Nehru** and **Sardar Vallabhbhai Patel**, focused on building political institutions,

promoting secularism, and addressing economic development in a country still recovering from the impacts of colonial rule.

Politics in the Modern World

Today, politics has evolved to encompass new dimensions—**globalization**, **technology**, and **climate change**—which have transformed how power is distributed and contested across nations. Political ideologies continue to shape governance systems, but new challenges like rising **authoritarianism**, **populism**, and **identity politics** have also redefined the political discourse.

As politics moves into the digital age, **social media**, **data** and **surveillance technologies** are reshaping political engagement, campaigning, and even voter manipulation, highlighting the complex and ever-evolving nature of power in the 21st century.

Power, Influence, and Decision-Making in Politics

Power, Influence, and Decision-Making in Politics

Politics, at its essence, revolves around power—who holds it, how it is exercised, and how it affects the lives of individuals and the structure of society. Understanding the dynamics of **power, influence**, and **decision-making** is crucial for grasping the intricacies of political systems, especially in complex and diverse societies like India.

Power and influence are interlinked, but they are not the same. Power refers to the ability to **control outcomes**, while influence refers to the **capacity to shape decisions or opinions** without direct control. In politics, both power and influence play pivotal roles in shaping governance, laws, and policies.

1. Understanding Power in Politics

Power is the central concept in political science and political theory. It is the means by which governments rule, laws are enforced, and societal order is maintained. However, power in politics goes beyond government control. It involves the ability to influence others and achieve desired outcomes through various mechanisms—authority, persuasion, negotiation, coercion, or force.

There are different types of political power that define how individuals, institutions, and groups interact within a political system:

1. **Legitimate Power**: This is power that is recognized as rightful by the people. In democracies, legitimate power is derived from the consent of the governed, typically through elections. Elected officials, like MPs and MLAs in India, hold legitimate power to make laws and policies on behalf of the public.

2. **Coercive Power**: Coercive power involves the use of force or threats to achieve compliance. This type of power is often seen in authoritarian regimes or during times of conflict, where governments use military or police force to maintain control or suppress dissent.

3. **Economic Power**: Economic power is wielded by those who control significant financial resources. In modern politics, economic power can be as influential as formal political authority. Corporations, wealthy individuals, and economic elites can shape political decisions through lobbying, funding political campaigns, or directly influencing policy-makers.

4. **Cultural and Ideological Power**: Cultural power is the ability to influence society's values, beliefs, and ideologies. In India, for instance, religion, caste, and regional identities play a significant role in shaping political power. Political leaders often harness cultural symbols and narratives to build influence and secure electoral victories.

5. **Informal Power**: Informal power refers to the influence exercised outside official institutions. Lobbyists, business leaders, social activists, and even celebrities can wield informal power. In India, power brokers and regional leaders who don't hold formal government positions still command significant influence in local or national politics.

6. **Soft Power**: A term popularized by political scientist **Joseph Nye**, soft power refers to the ability to influence others through attraction and persuasion rather than coercion. A country like India exercises soft power on the global stage through its culture, diplomacy, and democratic values.

2. Political Influence: How It Shapes Decisions

Political influence is about the ability to shape decisions or the political landscape without necessarily holding formal power. Influence in politics is often exerted through relationships, persuasion, or even manipulation.

1. **Lobbying and Interest Groups**: Lobbying is one of the most visible forms of influence in politics. It involves groups or individuals advocating for particular policies or decisions that favor their interests. For instance, agricultural lobbies in India have historically played a significant role in shaping agricultural policy, while corporate interests have influenced economic reforms, trade policies, and regulations.

2. **Media Influence**: Media plays a vital role in shaping public opinion, setting the political agenda, and holding leaders accountable. In the digital age, news channels, newspapers, and increasingly, social media platforms like Twitter and Facebook, are powerful tools for political influence. Political parties and movements can shape narratives, mobilize support, or even spread disinformation to influence decision-making and electoral outcomes.

3. **Civil Society and Social Movements**: Civil society organizations (CSOs) and grassroots movements are powerful agents of political influence. Movements such as the **Narmada Bachao Andolan** or more recently, the **Farmers' Protests** are examples of how citizens can mobilize and challenge government policies, influencing the political discourse. Such movements

often use public pressure, protests, petitions, and media campaigns to influence political decisions.

4. **Caste, Religion, and Identity**: In India, caste, religion, and regional identities remain potent sources of political influence. Political parties often cater to specific communities to build a loyal voter base. For example, caste-based parties like the **Bahujan Samaj Party (BSP)** or religiously oriented parties like the **Bharatiya Janata Party (BJP)**, which promotes a vision of Hindutva, exert immense influence by appealing to particular social groups.

5. **Social Media Influence**: In recent years, social media has emerged as a new frontier for political influence. Political campaigns are increasingly fought on digital platforms, where influencers, digital strategists, and even troll armies can shape public perception. In elections, politicians and parties use social media not only to reach voters but also to manipulate algorithms and promote specific content to boost their influence.

3. Decision-Making in Politics: The Process and Its Impact

Decision-making in politics involves a complex set of interactions between various stakeholders—government officials, political parties, civil society, and the public. Political decisions, whether they relate to economic policies, defense strategies, or social reforms, can have far-reaching consequences. Understanding the mechanisms of decision-making helps us appreciate how power and influence shape the outcomes of political processes.

1. **Institutional Decision-Making**: In democratic systems like India, the decision-making process typically involves various institutions—parliament, the judiciary, and the executive branch. Laws are proposed in **parliament** (Lok Sabha and Rajya Sabha), debated by representatives, and passed through a series of stages. The **executive**, led by the Prime Minister and the cabinet, is responsible for implementing these laws. The **ju-**

diciary, including the Supreme Court and High Courts, interprets laws and ensures that they align with the constitution.

2. **Policy-Making and Bureaucratic Influence**: Policy-making often involves bureaucrats and technocrats who draft, refine, and implement policies based on political direction. The Indian bureaucracy, while often seen as slow-moving, is a critical player in translating political decisions into actionable policies. Many decisions, from education reform to tax policies, are shaped by a combination of political priorities and bureaucratic expertise.

3. **Electoral Influence on Decision-Making**: Politicians in democracies are constantly mindful of electoral cycles. Decisions are often made with the next election in mind, leading to what is known as **populist politics**. This refers to short-term decisions made to appease the electorate rather than focusing on long-term national interests. For example, the announcement of **loan waivers** for farmers, especially before elections, is often seen as a populist measure aimed at securing votes.

4. **Public Opinion and Decision-Making**: In any democratic system, public opinion plays a key role in shaping political decisions. Governments often conduct **surveys**, assess **polls**, and monitor **media reactions** to gauge the public's sentiment on key issues. A government that ignores public opinion risks losing electoral support, as seen in instances where unpopular policies have led to large-scale protests or defeats at the ballot box.

5. **The Role of Political Parties**: Political parties are the primary drivers of decision-making in democratic systems. They shape policies, create party platforms, and make decisions about governance when they come to power. Party leaders and their inner circle typically make critical decisions, whether it's about forming coalitions, pushing through reforms, or even choosing electoral candidates. In India, the **Congress Party**, the **BJP**, and

regional parties like the **Trinamool Congress** or **DMK** play influential roles in shaping the political discourse.

6. **Checks and Balances**: In democratic systems, the principle of **checks and balances** ensures that no one branch of government becomes too powerful. In India, the **separation of powers** between the executive, legislature, and judiciary allows for oversight and accountability. Decisions made by the executive are subject to parliamentary debate, and if necessary, judicial review.

The interplay between **power**, **influence**, and **decision-making** in politics is essential to understanding the functioning of any political system. In India, where power is often contested between central and state governments, political parties, and various interest groups, these dynamics become even more complex. Political decisions can affect millions of lives, shape the economy, and determine the future trajectory of the nation. Thus, recognizing how power operates and how decisions are made provides crucial insight into the workings of India's democracy.

A Quick Overview of Political Ideologies

Political ideologies are the guiding principles behind how societies are governed, defining how power is distributed and how decisions are made. Understanding these ideologies is critical to making sense of political systems and their impact on everyday life. In India, with its rich diversity, a multitude of ideologies compete, influencing everything from policy-making to political campaigns.

Before diving into specific ideologies, it's important to start with the foundation of the Indian political system: **democracy**.

Democracy

Democracy is a system of government where power is vested in the hands of the people, who elect their representatives through free and fair elections. In a democracy, the rule of law prevails, and all citizens have equal rights. Freedom of speech, expression, and association are core principles, ensuring that people have a voice in how they are governed. Democracies can take many forms, but at their core, they seek to ensure the representation of the people's will through elected officials.

In India, democracy is a cornerstone of the Constitution, which guarantees a parliamentary system where leaders are elected by universal suffrage. India is the world's largest democracy, with regular elections allowing citizens to vote for representatives at the local, state, and national levels. Democratic institutions such as the **Election Commission of India** safeguard the integrity of the electoral process, ensuring that power transitions occur through peaceful means.

Now that we've established democracy as the foundation of the Indian political system, let's explore other political ideologies that shape how this democracy functions.

1. Conservatism

Conservatism is a political ideology that emphasizes tradition, social stability, and the importance of established institutions. Conservatives typically resist rapid change, preferring gradual reforms that maintain social order. They believe in preserving cultural heritage and upholding moral values rooted in historical traditions, often placing a high value on religion and national identity.

In India, conservative ideals are often linked with the promotion of cultural nationalism. The **Bharatiya Janata Party (BJP)**, which advocates a conservative political platform, emphasizes **Hindutva**, a form of Hindu nationalism, as well as a strong sense of Indian tradition and cultural identity. The conservative approach also advocates for economic liberalization and a limited role for government in economic affairs, reflecting free-market principles.

2. Liberalism

Liberalism is based on the values of individual freedom, human rights, and equality. Liberals advocate for political and civil rights, such as free speech, equality before the law, and the right to private property. Economic liberalism encourages free markets and limited government intervention in economic affairs, while social liberalism promotes government involvement to address social inequalities and protect individual freedoms.

In India, liberalism is represented by parties and politicians who advocate for economic reforms, freedom of the press, and individual rights. The **Indian National Congress (INC)**, historically, has leaned towards liberal policies, especially in terms of economic liberalization (beginning in the 1990s), as well as promoting secularism and democratic values.

3. Socialism

Socialism is a political ideology that advocates for social ownership of the means of production and wealth distribution to ensure economic equality. Socialists argue that the government should play a significant role in managing the economy, ensuring that wealth and resources are distributed more equitably among citizens. The idea behind socialism is to reduce the gap between the rich and the poor through state intervention, progressive taxation, and public services such as healthcare and education.

In India, socialist ideals have historically shaped the country's economic and social policies. After independence, leaders like **Jawaharlal Nehru** emphasized socialism through **planned economic development** and state ownership of key industries. Today, socialism continues to be part of the political dialogue, with parties like the **Communist Party of India (CPI)** and the **Samajwadi Party** advocating for policies that aim to uplift marginalized communities and reduce income inequality.

4. Communism

Communism is a more extreme form of socialism that advocates for the complete abolition of private property, with all means of production owned collectively by the people. In a communist society, wealth is distributed equally among all members, and there is no class hierarchy. Communism rejects the capitalist model of competition and profit, instead advocating for a classless, stateless society where wealth is distributed based on need.

In India, communism has had significant influence, especially in states like **West Bengal**, **Kerala**, and **Tripura**, where the **Communist Party of India (Marxist)** (CPI-M) has historically held power. These regions have seen land reforms, efforts to reduce rural poverty, and a focus on labor rights, consistent with communist principles.

5. Nationalism

Nationalism is the belief that a group of people sharing common history, culture, or language should govern themselves independently of foreign rule or outside influence. It emphasizes national pride, unity, and often involves the desire to preserve national sovereignty and cultural identity.

In India, nationalism has played a defining role in its political history. The fight for independence from British colonial rule was driven by a nationalist movement, which led to the creation of the Indian state. Today, nationalist ideologies manifest in various forms, such as **Hindutva**, which seeks to align India's identity with Hindu cultural values. Political parties like the **BJP** promote nationalist ideologies, emphasizing the importance of national sovereignty and a strong, centralized government.

6. Secularism

Secularism advocates for the separation of religion from the state, ensuring that no religious group is given preferential treatment in government policies or decisions. Secularism promotes equality for all citizens, regardless of their religious beliefs, and ensures that public institutions remain neutral in matters of faith.

In India, secularism is a key feature of the **Constitution**, which guarantees religious freedom and prohibits discrimination based on religion. However, the implementation of secularism in Indian politics has often been debated, particularly given the country's deep religious diversity. The **Indian National Congress** has traditionally championed secularism, though the concept is often contested in modern political discourse, particularly in light of growing religious polarization.

7. Populism

Populism is a political approach that seeks to appeal to the common people, often by contrasting them against the elites or the establishment. Populist leaders claim to represent the will of the majority and often frame their political message in terms of the "people" versus the "elite." Populism can be found across the political spectrum, whether left or right.

In India, populist policies have been a hallmark of many political campaigns. Leaders often appeal to large sections of the population by offering immediate benefits, such as **loan waivers**, **subsidized food**, or **free electricity**. Populism can sometimes be associated with **election-time promises** that offer short-term benefits to gain votes but may not focus on long-term solutions.

8. Anarchism

Anarchism is the belief in the abolition of all government and the establishment of a society based on voluntary cooperation and free association of individuals. Anarchists reject hierarchical structures, whether in politics, economics, or social institutions, and advocate for a society where people govern themselves without any formal authority.

In India, anarchism has not been a prominent political ideology in mainstream politics. However, anarchist elements can sometimes be seen in movements that reject the authority of the state, particularly in regions with insurgencies or among groups that feel excluded from the political system.

9. Environmentalism

Environmentalism is a political ideology that prioritizes the protection and preservation of the natural environment. Environmentalists advocate for sustainable development, the conservation of natural resources, and the mitigation of climate change. This ideology has gained significant traction in recent years due to increasing environmental degradation and the growing threat of climate change.

In India, environmentalism has become increasingly important, with many political leaders and civil society groups advocating for policies that address environmental concerns. Movements like the **Chipko Movement** or recent protests against large-scale industrial projects that harm the environment are rooted in environmentalism. Political parties such as the **Aam Aadmi Party (AAP)** have also integrated environmental concerns into their platforms, advocating for clean air, water conservation, and sustainable energy.

10. Feminism

Feminism is a political ideology that advocates for gender equality and the rights of women. Feminists work to address issues such as gender discrimination, workplace inequality, reproductive rights, and violence against women. The feminist movement seeks to challenge patriarchal systems that have historically marginalized women and seeks greater representation for women in politics, business, and society at large.

In India, feminism has played a significant role in advancing women's rights. Movements such as the fight for **women's reservation in parliament**, campaigns against **domestic violence**, and the push for gender-sensitive laws, like the **Vishakha Guidelines** against sexual harassment, are rooted in feminist ideals. Feminist movements in India have also fought for better representation of women in politics and leadership positions.

Each political ideology provides a different lens through which we can view governance, societal structure, and individual rights. Understanding these ideologies helps citizens make informed decisions during elections, assess government policies, and engage meaningfully in political discourse. In a country as diverse as India, with its multitude of political parties and movements, these ideologies play a crucial role in shaping the future of the nation.

Conclusion: Political Ideologies in India's Context

India's political landscape is a unique blend of different ideologies. The **Constitution of India** draws from multiple political philosophies—democratic, socialist, and capitalist—creating a system that aims to balance the **freedom of individuals with the welfare of society as a whole**.

Understanding these political ideologies helps us make sense of the different political parties and movements in India. The **Indian National Congress** has traditionally leaned toward **democratic socialism**, while the **Bharatiya Janata Party (BJP)** embraces a more **right-wing, capitalist approach. Communist parties** still retain influence in some regions, and regional parties often mix ideologies based on local needs.

As young citizens of India, understanding these different ideologies helps you engage more effectively with the political system. You will better understand how different political parties operate, what their goals are, and how their policies impact your life. This understanding will also enable you to make informed decisions during elections and take part in political discussions that shape the future of India.

In the chapters ahead, we will dive deeper into how these ideologies manifest in India's governance, policies, and political structures, offering you a comprehensive understanding of the forces that shape our nation.

| 3 |

The Indian Political System

India, the world's largest democracy, has a unique and multifaceted political system that governs over 1.4 billion people from diverse cultural, linguistic, and ethnic backgrounds. Understanding this system is key to grasping how decisions are made and how power is distributed in the country. This chapter will explore the foundational principles of the Indian political system, including the **Constitution**, the **Parliament and Legislative Assemblies**, and the **election process**.

The Constitution of India: Backbone of Indian Democracy

The **Constitution of India** is the foundation of the world's largest democracy, setting the framework for governance, law, and the rights and duties of its citizens. Drafted after India gained independence from British rule, the Constitution was adopted on **26th November 1949** and came into effect on **26th January 1950**, marking India's transition to a sovereign republic. It serves not only as a legal document but also as a symbol of India's democratic ethos, guiding the nation's political, social, and economic progress.

The Making of the Constitution

The process of drafting the Indian Constitution was a historic task led by a Constituent Assembly, which was formed in **1946**. The assembly consisted of **299 members**, representing a wide range of political ideologies, religious communities, and social groups. Under the leadership of **Dr. B.R. Ambedkar**, the **Chairman of the Drafting Committee**, and other notable leaders like **Jawaharlal Nehru, Sardar Vallabhbhai Patel, and Maulana Abul Kalam Azad**, the assembly worked tirelessly to create a document that reflected the aspirations of a newly independent nation.

The Indian Constitution drew inspiration from several global sources, including the **British parliamentary system**, the **U.S. Bill of Rights**, the **Irish Directive Principles of State Policy**, and the **Canadian federal structure**. However, the final product was uniquely Indian, tailored to the country's cultural, linguistic, and religious diversity. The Constitution was designed to ensure that India would remain a secular, democratic republic that upheld the values of **justice, liberty, equality**, and **fraternity**.

Salient Features of the Indian Constitution

1. **Length and Detail** The Indian Constitution is the **longest written constitution in the world**, with **448 articles** divided into **25 parts, 12 schedules**, and over **100 amendments** (as of 2024). Its comprehensive nature allows for detailed provisions on various aspects of governance, including the structure of the government, the judiciary, elections, and the rights of citizens. The length also reflects the framers' effort to address the complexity and diversity of the Indian population.

2. **Preamble: A Vision for India** The **Preamble** of the Constitution outlines the guiding principles of the nation: India is a **sovereign, socialist, secular, and democratic republic**. It pledges to secure **justice, liberty, equality**, and promote **fraternity** among its citizens. The preamble serves as a mission statement for the Constitution, encapsulating the values that guide India's governance and society.

3. **Federalism with a Unitary Bias** The Constitution establishes India as a **federal state**, meaning power is shared between the **central (or union) government** and the **state governments**.

However, it also has a **unitary bias**, granting the central government more power in times of crisis or national emergency. The **Seventh Schedule** of the Constitution outlines the division of powers through three lists: the **Union List**, the **State List**, and the **Concurrent List**, ensuring a balance between state autonomy and central authority.

4. **Parliamentary System of Government** India follows the **parliamentary system** of government, similar to that of the United Kingdom. The **President of India** is the ceremonial head of state, while the **Prime Minister** is the head of government and holds real executive power. The **Parliament of India** is a **bicameral legislature**, consisting of the **Lok Sabha (House of the People)** and the **Rajya Sabha (Council of States)**. Laws are made through a collaborative process between the two houses and the President, with the **executive branch** accountable to the legislature.

5. **Fundamental Rights and Duties** One of the most significant parts of the Indian Constitution is the section on **Fundamental Rights** (Part III), which guarantees basic freedoms and protections to all citizens. These include:

6. **Right to Equality** (Article 14–18): Equality before the law and prohibition of discrimination.

7. **Right to Freedom** (Article 19–22): Freedom of speech, expression, assembly, association, movement, and residence.

8. **Right against Exploitation** (Article 23–24): Prohibition of human trafficking, forced labor, and child labor.

9. **Right to Freedom of Religion** (Article 25–28): Freedom to practice, profess, and propagate any religion.

10. **Cultural and Educational Rights** (Article 29–30): Protection of cultural, linguistic, and religious minorities.

11. **Right to Constitutional Remedies** (Article 32): The right to approach the courts for enforcement of Fundamental Rights.

12. Additionally, the **Fundamental Duties** (added by the 42nd Amendment in 1976) remind citizens of their responsibilities,

such as respecting the Constitution, promoting harmony, and safeguarding public property.

13. **Directive Principles of State Policy** The **Directive Principles of State Policy** (Part IV) are guidelines for the government to follow in the governance of the country. Although these principles are non-justiciable (meaning they cannot be enforced in a court of law), they are crucial for the establishment of social and economic democracy. These principles aim to promote the welfare of the people by securing a just social order, reducing income inequalities, and providing access to basic needs such as education and healthcare.

14. **Secularism** The Indian Constitution declares India a **secular state**, meaning there is no official state religion. The government does not favor any religion, and all citizens are free to practice, propagate, and profess their religion without fear of discrimination. This principle is particularly important in a country as religiously diverse as India.

15. **Independent Judiciary** The Constitution guarantees an **independent judiciary**, which acts as a guardian of the Constitution and the fundamental rights of the people. The **Supreme Court of India** is the highest court in the country, with the power of **judicial review**, allowing it to strike down laws that are unconstitutional. The judiciary is designed to act as a check on the powers of the executive and the legislature, ensuring the rule of law is upheld.

16. **Amendability** The framers of the Constitution recognized that it needed to be flexible enough to adapt to changing circumstances, but also stable enough to prevent frequent or arbitrary changes. **Article 368** outlines the procedure for amending the Constitution. Amendments require a special majority in Parliament and, in some cases, the consent of at least half of the state legislatures. This balance ensures the Constitution evolves with time without losing its foundational principles.

17. **Emergency Provisions** The Constitution includes provisions for declaring a **national emergency** (Article 352), **state emergency** (Article 356), and **financial emergency** (Article 360). These provisions allow for the temporary suspension of certain rights and a shift of power from the states to the center in times of crisis. While emergency powers are essential for national security and stability, their misuse has been a matter of controversy, most notably during the **Emergency of 1975-1977**.

The Role of the Constitution in Modern Indian Politics

The Constitution of India continues to be the guiding force behind Indian politics and governance. It provides a framework within which political parties operate, elections are conducted, and governance is executed. Despite challenges like corruption, religious polarization, and regional disparities, the Constitution remains a beacon of **democratic governance** and **rule of law**.

Constitutional amendments, such as the **73rd and 74th Amendments** empowering local governance through **Panchayati Raj** institutions and **urban local bodies**, demonstrate the Constitution's flexibility in adapting to the needs of modern India. Similarly, landmark judicial interpretations of the Constitution, such as the **basic structure doctrine**, safeguard its core principles from arbitrary amendments.

In an era of rapid change, where social media, digital governance, and globalization are transforming the political landscape, the Constitution remains the backbone of Indian democracy. It not only ensures the functioning of government institutions but also protects the rights and freedoms of over **1.4 billion citizens**, making it a living document that continues to evolve with the aspirations of the Indian people.

Parliament and Legislative Assemblies: National and State Governance

India's governance structure is built on the principles of **federalism**, which divides powers between the **central (union) government** and **state governments**. At the heart of this system are two key institutions: the **Parliament of India**, which is responsible for national governance, and the **Legislative Assemblies**, which handle governance at the state level. Together, these institutions ensure that laws, policies, and administrative decisions are made at both the national and state levels, enabling a balance between central authority and state autonomy.

Parliament of India: National Governance

The **Parliament of India** is the supreme legislative body of the country and operates at the national level. It is a **bicameral legislature**, meaning it consists of two houses: the **Lok Sabha (House of the People)** and the **Rajya Sabha (Council of States)**. The two houses together are responsible for making laws, passing budgets, and holding the government accountable to the people of India. The system is designed to ensure both representation by population (in the Lok Sabha) and representation by states (in the Rajya Sabha), reflecting the country's federal structure.

1. **Lok Sabha (House of the People)** The **Lok Sabha** is the lower house of Parliament and the directly elected chamber. It represents the people of India as a whole. Members of the Lok Sabha (MPs) are elected by the people of India through general elections held every **five years**. The number of seats in the Lok Sabha is based on population, with a total of **543 elected members** (as of 2024). Each MP represents a specific geographical area called a **constituency**, and the party (or coalition of parties) with a majority of seats forms the government.

2. **Prime Minister and the Executive** The **Prime Minister of India**, who is the head of the government, is usually the leader of the majority party in the Lok Sabha. The Prime Minis-

ter, along with the **Council of Ministers**, exercises executive power and is responsible for running the country's day-to-day affairs. However, they remain accountable to the Lok Sabha, which can remove the government through a vote of no confidence.

3. **Legislative Role** The primary function of the Lok Sabha is to introduce and pass legislation. Any bill related to national policies, taxation, finance, or governance must first be introduced in the Lok Sabha. The Lok Sabha debates, amends, and votes on bills, which, once approved, move to the Rajya Sabha for further consideration.

4. **Money Bills** One key distinction of the Lok Sabha is its exclusive authority to introduce **money bills**—those that deal with taxation, government expenditure, and financial matters. The Rajya Sabha can only make recommendations on money bills, but the Lok Sabha has the final say.

5. **Rajya Sabha (Council of States)** The **Rajya Sabha** is the upper house of Parliament and represents the states and union territories of India. It consists of **245 members**, with most members being elected by the elected members of the **State Legislative Assemblies** using a proportional representation system. A small number of members are nominated by the **President of India** for their expertise in fields like literature, science, art, or social service.

6. **Federal Balance** The Rajya Sabha plays a crucial role in ensuring the federal balance by representing the interests of the states. Its members are indirectly elected, giving state legislatures a voice in the national legislative process. This feature allows states to have input on laws and policies that may affect their rights and autonomy.

7. **Legislative Review** The Rajya Sabha serves as a **reviewing body**, acting as a check on the directly elected Lok Sabha. While it cannot reject money bills, it can delay other types of legislation, propose amendments, and engage in meaningful

debate, ensuring that laws passed by the Lok Sabha undergo thorough scrutiny before becoming law.

8. **Tenure and Permanency** Unlike the Lok Sabha, which is dissolved every five years, the Rajya Sabha is a **permanent body**. Its members have a tenure of **six years**, with one-third of its members retiring every two years. This staggered system ensures that the Rajya Sabha remains a continuous body, providing stability and continuity to the legislative process.

9. **Role of the President of India** The **President of India** is the ceremonial head of state and plays a key role in the legislative process. All bills passed by Parliament must receive the President's assent to become law. While the President's role is largely ceremonial, they have the power to send a bill back to Parliament for reconsideration (except for money bills) and can also summon or dissolve the Lok Sabha based on the advice of the Prime Minister and the Council of Ministers.

Legislative Assemblies: State Governance

At the state level, governance is carried out through **Legislative Assemblies**, which are the elected law-making bodies for each state. Just as the Lok Sabha represents the people at the national level, Legislative Assemblies represent the people at the state level, making laws that pertain to state-specific issues and needs. State governments handle issues like public health, education, agriculture, and local infrastructure.

1. **Vidhan Sabha (Legislative Assembly)** The **Vidhan Sabha** is the lower house of the state legislature in states with a bicameral system (e.g., Uttar Pradesh, Maharashtra, Bihar) or the sole legislative body in states with a unicameral system (e.g., Kerala, Punjab). Members of the Vidhan Sabha are directly elected by the people of the state through elections held every **five years**. The number of members varies depending on the population and size of the state.

2. **Chief Minister and State Executive** The **Chief Minister** is the head of the government in a state and leads the **Council of Ministers**. Like the Prime Minister at the national level, the Chief Minister is responsible for the administration of the state and is accountable to the Vidhan Sabha. The Chief Minister and their ministers implement policies, enforce laws, and manage state finances.

3. **State Legislation** The Vidhan Sabha's primary function is to legislate on matters listed in the **State List** and **Concurrent List** of the Constitution. These include areas such as agriculture, police, healthcare, and local governance. The Vidhan Sabha also holds the state government accountable, approves the state budget, and debates issues affecting the state's development.

4. **Money Bills and Financial Powers** Similar to the Lok Sabha, the Vidhan Sabha has exclusive powers to introduce and pass **money bills** related to state finances, taxation, and expenditure. However, for non-financial matters, the state's **Governor** must give assent to any bills passed by the Vidhan Sabha for them to become law.

5. **Vidhan Parishad (Legislative Council)** In some states, like Bihar, Maharashtra, and Karnataka, there is an upper house called the **Vidhan Parishad** or Legislative Council. Members of the Vidhan Parishad are not directly elected by the people; they are either elected by members of the Vidhan Sabha or appointed by the Governor. The Vidhan Parishad serves a similar role to the Rajya Sabha at the state level, providing a platform for more detailed legislative review and debate.

6. **Review and Advisory Role** The Vidhan Parishad can review, suggest amendments, or delay legislation passed by the Vidhan Sabha but cannot block the passage of money bills. Its members often include experts in various fields, contributing to a more informed and nuanced legislative process.

7. **Permanent Body** Like the Rajya Sabha, the Vidhan Parishad is a permanent body, with members serving staggered terms of six years, ensuring continuity in the state's legislative process.

Division of Powers: Union, State, and Concurrent Lists

The **Seventh Schedule** of the Indian Constitution clearly outlines the division of powers between the union and state governments. These powers are divided into three lists:

1. **Union List**: This includes subjects of national importance such as defense, foreign affairs, atomic energy, banking, and communication. The central government has exclusive authority over these matters.
2. **State List**: This includes subjects of local or state importance such as police, public health, agriculture, and local government. State governments have exclusive authority over these subjects, allowing them to legislate according to the specific needs of their population.
3. **Concurrent List**: This includes subjects like education, criminal law, forests, and marriage. Both the union and state governments can make laws on these subjects. In case of a conflict, the law passed by the union government prevails.

Thus, the Indian system of government, with its intricate balance between the **Parliament** and **Legislative Assemblies**, reflects the federal nature of the country. It allows both the **central government** and **state governments** to operate effectively, each addressing issues relevant to their level of governance. The structure ensures that India remains a union of states with shared powers, while also preserving the rights of states to legislate on matters that directly affect their citizens.

This system of checks and balances is vital in maintaining **democratic governance** in India, ensuring that power is not concentrated in any single institution and that governance is responsive to the diverse needs of its people.

The Election Process

The **election process** is the cornerstone of India's **democratic system**, providing a mechanism for the people to choose their representatives at various levels of government. As the world's largest democracy, India conducts elections that are complex, vast, and highly organized. The country's election process is designed to be free, fair, and transparent, ensuring that all citizens, regardless of social or economic standing, can exercise their **right to vote**.

This section will provide a comprehensive overview of how elections are conducted in India, covering the key stages and elements that make up the election process, from voter registration to the declaration of results. It will also touch upon the roles of various institutions and key players that ensure the integrity of the electoral system.

1. The Role of the Election Commission of India

The **Election Commission of India (ECI)** is the central body responsible for overseeing and conducting elections in the country. It is an autonomous and independent institution established under **Article 324** of the Indian Constitution. The ECI ensures that elections are conducted impartially and in accordance with the law.

Key functions of the ECI include:

- **Administering elections** for the **Lok Sabha, Rajya Sabha, State Legislative Assemblies**, and **State Legislative Councils**.
- Conducting elections for the offices of the **President** and **Vice President of India**.
- Delimiting constituencies and preparing **electoral rolls**.
- Monitoring campaign finance, expenditure, and the use of government machinery during elections.

- Enforcing the **Model Code of Conduct**, which is a set of guidelines for political parties and candidates during the election period.
- Declaring election dates and ensuring all logistics are in place for smooth conduct of elections.

The independence of the ECI is crucial to the integrity of India's electoral process, ensuring that elections remain free from undue influence and that citizens have confidence in the system.

2. Voter Eligibility and Registration

To participate in elections, citizens of India must meet specific eligibility criteria:

- Be at least **18 years of age** on the qualifying date, as defined by the **Representation of the People Act, 1950**.
- Be a citizen of India.
- Be registered as a voter in the constituency in which they reside.

The process of **voter registration** is essential to ensure that every eligible citizen is able to vote. The ECI periodically updates the **electoral roll**, and citizens can register either during these updates or individually online. Voter identification is essential on the day of voting, and the ECI issues **Voter ID cards** to all registered voters. Additionally, other approved forms of identification, such as Aadhaar cards or passports, can also be used.

3. Constituencies and Representation

India's election process is based on the concept of **territorial representation**, where the country is divided into smaller geographical units called **constituencies**. Each constituency elects one representative to a legislative body, ensuring local representation in both national and state governments.

- **Lok Sabha Constituencies**: India is divided into **543 constituencies** for Lok Sabha elections, each electing one Member of Parliament (MP). These constituencies are based on population, with adjustments made periodically through a process known as **delimitation**.
- **State Legislative Assembly Constituencies**: Similar to the Lok Sabha, each state is divided into constituencies for its **Legislative Assembly elections**, and voters from each constituency elect one Member of the Legislative Assembly (MLA). The number of constituencies per state varies depending on its population.

Delimitation of constituencies ensures that representation remains equitable as population densities shift, although this process has been frozen until **2026**.

4. Election Campaigning

Election campaigning is the period when political parties and candidates actively engage with the public, presenting their platforms, policies, and promises in an effort to secure votes. Campaigning involves rallies, speeches, media appearances, social media engagement, and door-to-door canvassing.

Political parties typically release their **manifestos**, which outline their vision and policies on key national or state issues. The campaign period is also when the **Model Code of Conduct** comes into play, outlining rules that candidates and parties must follow to ensure that the election is conducted ethically and without unfair advantages. This includes guidelines on how government resources should be used, how candidates interact with voters, and restrictions on campaign spending.

5. Voting Methods and Election Day

The most crucial part of the election process is **voting**. India uses a **first-past-the-post system** for both the **Lok Sabha** and **State Legislative Assembly** elections. This means that the candidate who receives the highest number of votes in a constituency wins, even if they do not secure an absolute majority.

- **Polling Booths and Election Day**: On **election day**, voters are required to cast their vote at designated **polling stations** within their constituency. Polling stations are set up in various locations such as schools, community centers, and government offices. Voting is typically conducted over several phases to manage the vast number of voters and ensure security, especially in sensitive regions.
- **Electronic Voting Machines (EVMs)**: Since **2004**, India has used **Electronic Voting Machines (EVMs)** to streamline the voting process and reduce the chances of tampering with physical ballots. EVMs allow voters to simply press a button next to their preferred candidate's name, ensuring both speed and accuracy in counting votes. The **Voter Verifiable Paper Audit Trail (VVPAT)** system was introduced in 2013 to provide a paper record of votes, enhancing transparency.
- **Postal and Proxy Voting**: For those unable to physically attend a polling station, such as military personnel, the option of **postal voting** or **proxy voting** is available. In recent years, discussions about **e-voting** (online voting) have also gained traction, particularly as a way to encourage greater participation among expatriate Indians and disabled citizens.

6. Vote Counting and Declaration of Results

After the voting process is completed, **vote counting** begins under the supervision of the ECI. The process is transparent, and representatives from all political parties are allowed to observe the counting to prevent any malpractice.

- **Counting Process**: Votes are counted constituency by constituency. The results from each EVM are tallied, and the candidate with the highest number of votes is declared the winner.

The counting process is closely monitored, and any discrepancies can be addressed by the ECI.

- **Declaration of Results**: Once the counting is complete, the results are declared. The party (or coalition) that secures the most seats forms the government, with the leader of the winning party becoming either the **Prime Minister** at the national level or the **Chief Minister** at the state level.

7. Challenges and Reforms in the Election Process

India's election process is a mammoth undertaking, but it is not without challenges. **Corruption**, **vote-buying**, and **criminalization of politics** remain significant issues, especially at the local level. Furthermore, **electoral violence** and **booth capturing** have been reported in certain regions, although these have been mitigated in recent years by strict enforcement of laws and the presence of security forces.

Efforts to introduce **electoral reforms** are ongoing. Proposals for reforms include:

- **Simultaneous Elections**: A proposal to conduct national and state elections simultaneously to reduce costs and election fatigue.
- **Transparency in Party Funding**: Increasing transparency in how political parties receive and spend money during campaigns.
- **E-voting**: Introducing secure online voting systems to make voting more accessible.

The **election process** in India is a testament to the strength and complexity of its democracy. Through periodic, free, and fair elections, citizens are empowered to choose their representatives and hold them accountable. While challenges remain, India's electoral system continues to evolve, incorporating technology and reforms to make it more inclusive, transparent, and efficient.

Conclusion: The Heart of Indian Democracy

The Indian political system is vast, complex, and dynamic, shaped by centuries of history, culture, and political thought. At its core, the system is designed to give power to the people through **democratic processes** and **constitutional guarantees**. However, it is also a system that faces many challenges, including corruption, electoral manipulation, and the need for ongoing reforms.

As we move forward in this book, we will dive deeper into how this political system affects various aspects of life in India, from **economic policies** to **social welfare**. Understanding the Constitution, the role of Parliament, and the election process is the first step toward becoming an informed and engaged citizen. With this knowledge, young readers will be better equipped to participate in the democratic process and shape the future of India.

| 4 |

Political Parties in India

Political parties are the cornerstone of any democracy, and in India, they play a particularly vital role due to the country's vast diversity and large population. The political landscape in India has undergone several changes since independence, with the rise of both national and regional parties, coalition governments, and the growing influence of money in politics. This chapter provides an in-depth look at the **evolution of political parties**, the dynamics of **coalition politics**, and the critical issue of **party funding**. We'll also briefly compare the Indian party system with other democracies like the **US** and **UK**.

The Rise and Evolution of Political Parties in India

India's political landscape is deeply intertwined with the history and evolution of its **political parties**. Political parties in India are the lifeblood of the democratic system, serving as the primary vehicles for organizing political activity, contesting elections, and forming governments. The rise and evolution of political parties in India reflect the nation's complex history, diverse society, and dynamic political movements.

1. Pre-Independence Era: The Birth of Political Movements

The roots of political parties in India can be traced back to the **pre-independence era**, during the British colonial rule. Political organizations were primarily formed as movements to challenge British authority, demand reforms, and advocate for India's self-rule. The **Indian National Congress (INC)**, formed in 1885, became the most significant political force during this period, representing various Indian communities in their struggle for independence.

The INC began as a platform for **elite Indians** to voice their concerns to the British government, but it gradually transformed into a mass political movement under leaders like **Mahatma Gandhi**, **Jawaharlal Nehru**, **Sardar Vallabhbhai Patel**, and **Subhas Chandra Bose**. With its strategy of **non-violence** and **civil disobedience**, the INC galvanized support across different sections of Indian society, leading the charge for India's independence in 1947.

However, the INC was not the only party active during the freedom struggle. Other political groups, such as the **Muslim League**, emerged, representing specific communities or ideologies. The Muslim League, led by **Muhammad Ali Jinnah**, played a crucial role in advocating for the creation of **Pakistan**, which eventually led to the **partition of India** in 1947.

2. Post-Independence Era: The Dominance of the Congress Party

After India gained independence, the **Indian National Congress** became the dominant political force in the country. Under the leadership of **Jawaharlal Nehru**, who became India's first Prime Minister, the Congress Party set the agenda for the nation's political, social, and economic policies. The INC's role in leading the independence movement gave it unparalleled credibility and support from across the country.

During the early years of independence, the Congress Party operated as a broad-based, centrist party that aimed to represent all sections of Indian society, from the urban elite to rural farmers and the working class. The party pursued **socialist-inspired policies**, focusing on state-led industrialization, land reforms, and the creation of a **mixed economy**. The Congress maintained its dominance through the 1950s and 1960s, winning successive elections and holding a strong majority in the **Lok Sabha** (the lower house of Parliament).

However, as the Congress Party grew more powerful, internal factions began to emerge. Different ideological streams within the party — ranging from **left-wing socialists** to **right-leaning conservatives** — began to challenge the unity of the Congress. Moreover, the party's dominance also led to accusations of **corruption**, **authoritarianism**, and **complacency**.

3. The Rise of Regional and Opposition Parties (1960s–1980s)

By the late 1960s, cracks in the Congress's dominance began to appear. One of the most significant challenges to the INC came from the **split within the party** itself. In 1969, the Congress split into two factions — the **Congress (O)**, led by older conservative leaders, and **Congress (R)**, led by **Indira Gandhi**, Nehru's daughter. Indira Gandhi, known for her populist politics, rebranded Congress as a pro-poor, socialist party, which won her significant support from the masses.

However, the period of the 1970s was marked by political upheaval and the rise of opposition parties. Indira Gandhi's declaration of **Emergency** in 1975, where democratic rights were suspended, led to widespread disillusionment with the Congress. This allowed opposition parties to come together under the **Janata Party** banner, forming India's first non-Congress government in 1977. The **Janata Party** represented a coalition of socialists, conservatives, and regional interests, signaling the growing importance of **regional and caste-based parties** in Indian politics.

The 1980s also saw the emergence of **regional parties**, particularly in states with distinct linguistic, cultural, or economic identities. Parties like the **Dravida Munnetra Kazhagam (DMK)** and **All India Anna Dravida Munnetra Kazhagam (AIADMK)** in Tamil Nadu, **Shiv Sena** in Maharashtra, **Akali Dal** in Punjab, and **Telugu Desam Party (TDP)** in Andhra Pradesh began to assert themselves, challenging the Congress's hold over these states. These regional parties catered to local interests and often capitalized on regional pride, economic concerns, or cultural identity.

4. The BJP and the Rise of Hindutva Politics (1980s–2000s)

One of the most significant political developments in post-independence India was the rise of the **Bharatiya Janata Party (BJP)**. The BJP evolved from the **Jana Sangh**, a Hindu nationalist party that had been active since the 1950s. In 1980, the **Rashtriya Swayamsevak Sangh (RSS)**, a Hindu nationalist organization, helped form the BJP, which embraced the ideology of **Hindutva** — the promotion of Hindu values and culture as the foundation of Indian identity.

Throughout the 1980s, the BJP began to grow in popularity, particularly in the Hindi-speaking belt of northern India. The party's breakthrough came with its involvement in the **Ram Janmabhoomi movement**, which advocated for the construction of a temple dedicated to the Hindu god Ram at the site of the **Babri Masjid** in Ayodhya. The demolition of the Babri Masjid in 1992 sparked communal violence across the country, but it also helped the BJP consolidate its **Hindu nationalist base**.

By the late 1990s, the BJP emerged as a dominant national party, forming a coalition government under **Atal Bihari Vajpayee** in 1998. The BJP's rise signaled a significant shift in Indian politics, with the Congress Party no longer enjoying an unchallenged monopoly on power. The BJP's emphasis on **Hindutva**, **economic liberalization**, and **strong leadership** resonated with a large section of the Indian population, particularly the growing urban middle class.

5. Coalition Politics and the Decline of Single-Party Dominance (1990s–2000s)

With the rise of both the BJP and regional parties, Indian politics entered a phase of **coalition governance** in the 1990s. No single party was able to secure a clear majority in the Lok Sabha elections, leading to the formation of multi-party coalitions. Both the Congress and the BJP had to rely on alliances with regional and smaller parties to form governments.

This period marked the decline of single-party dominance in India, and the political landscape became increasingly fragmented. Coalitions like the **National Democratic Alliance (NDA)**, led by the BJP, and the **United Progressive Alliance (UPA)**, led by Congress, became the new norm in Indian politics. Coalition politics brought more voices and interests into the national government, but it also made governance more complex and sometimes unstable.

6. The Present-Day Political Scenario (2010s–2020s)

The **2014 general election** marked a turning point in Indian politics. The BJP, under the leadership of **Narendra Modi**, won a sweeping victory, securing an outright majority in the Lok Sabha — the first time this had happened in over 30 years. Modi's campaign focused on **economic development**, **good governance**, and **Hindu nationalism**, and his personal charisma played a significant role in the BJP's victory.

Since 2014, the BJP has continued to expand its influence, winning several state elections and consolidating its position as the dominant party at the national level. Meanwhile, the Congress Party, once the dominant force in Indian politics, has struggled to regain its footing, suffering from leadership crises and electoral defeats.

The present political landscape in India is characterized by:

- The dominance of the **BJP** at the national level.
- The persistence of **regional parties** that hold power in states like Tamil Nadu, West Bengal, and Odisha.
- The continuing role of **coalition politics** in many state governments.
- The rising use of **social media** and **technology** in political campaigns, significantly reshaping how elections are fought.

The Dynamic Nature of Indian Political Parties

The rise and evolution of political parties in India are emblematic of the nation's democratic vibrancy. From the **Congress Party's** dominance in the early decades to the rise of **regional parties** and the

BJP's current hegemony, Indian political parties have evolved to reflect the changing aspirations, identities, and concerns of its diverse population.

Political parties in India will continue to evolve, responding to the pressures of economic development, social justice, identity politics, and the ever-changing global political environment. The success of any political party lies in its ability to connect with the people and address the challenges of contemporary India, ensuring that the country's democracy remains robust and representative of its citizens' diverse interests.

Coalition Politics: How Coalitions Work and Their Role in Forming Governments

India's political landscape has evolved significantly over the years, and one of the most defining aspects of its modern electoral system is **coalition politics**. This system has been shaped by the diversity of the country, both in terms of its geography and the interests of its population, resulting in a multiparty democracy where no single party often wins an outright majority. Coalition politics, therefore, has become a critical mechanism for governance at both the **national** and **state levels**.

1. What is Coalition Politics?

In simple terms, **coalition politics** refers to the practice of two or more political parties coming together to form a government. When no single party secures an outright majority in the **Lok Sabha** (the lower house of India's Parliament) or a state legislative assembly, parties may need to form alliances or coalitions to command the required majority to govern.

Coalitions are usually the result of **pre-election alliances** or **post-election negotiations**. Pre-election alliances occur when parties come together before elections, presenting a united front to voters. Post-election coalitions are formed when election results yield a hung assembly or parliament, prompting different parties to join hands to reach the magic number required for governance.

India's coalition politics gained prominence in the 1980s and 1990s as the political landscape became more fragmented with the rise of **regional parties** and the declining dominance of the **Indian National Congress (INC)**. Since then, coalition governments have been the norm rather than the exception.

2. The Need for Coalition Governments in India

India's **multiparty system** is a product of its diverse social, cultural, linguistic, and regional identities. This diversity is mirrored in the nation's electoral system, where numerous political parties—both national and regional—compete for votes. As India matured as a democracy, regional issues became increasingly significant, leading to the rise of **regional parties** that represent the specific interests of various states or communities.

Given the sheer size and complexity of India, it is increasingly difficult for a single party to address all of these diverse interests effectively. As a result, no single party has consistently managed to win a **majority** in general elections, especially at the national level, making coalitions a necessity.

Coalitions allow parties to pool their resources and support bases, bringing together different ideological, regional, and interest-based groups under one umbrella for the sake of governance. This process allows governments to reflect the multifaceted nature of India's electorate, making the governance structure more inclusive, although it can also introduce challenges related to maintaining unity within the coalition.

3. Pre-Election Alliances vs. Post-Election Coalitions

In coalition politics, two main approaches exist: **pre-election alliances** and **post-election coalitions**.

Pre-Election Alliances: In a pre-election alliance, political parties come together before elections are held. They share resources, pool votes, and often negotiate the sharing of constituencies (deciding which party will contest from which seat). A classic example of a pre-election alliance is the **National Democratic Alliance (NDA)**, led by the **Bharatiya Janata Party (BJP)**, and the **United Progressive Alliance (UPA)**, led by the **Indian National Congress (INC)**. Pre-election alliances allow parties to enter the polls with a unified platform and campaign, increasing their chances of collectively securing a majority.

Post-Election Coalitions: If no party or pre-election alliance secures a majority after the election results are announced, political parties may need to form **post-election coalitions**. In these coalitions, negotiations are held after the election to bring together parties with sufficient seats to form a governing majority. A post-election coalition often involves intense bargaining over cabinet positions, policy agreements, and shared power.

4. The Role of Regional Parties in Coalition Politics

One of the most critical elements of coalition politics in India is the role played by **regional parties**. While national parties like the **BJP** and the **Congress** dominate the national stage, regional parties often hold considerable power at the state level. In many cases, these regional parties become **kingmakers** in the formation of coalition governments, especially when the results lead to a hung parliament or assembly.

For example, in states like **West Bengal**, **Tamil Nadu**, **Andhra Pradesh**, and **Uttar Pradesh**, regional parties such as the **Trinamool Congress (TMC)**, **Dravida Munnetra Kazhagam (DMK)**, **Telugu Desam Party (TDP)**, and **Samajwadi Party (SP)** have significant influence. These parties often secure a substantial number of seats in their states and can tip the balance of power in coalition negotiations.

Regional parties bring localized concerns to national politics. They advocate for the interests of their specific states, whether it is related to **development projects**, **economic reforms**, or **cultural preservation**. As a result, coalition governments often have to accommodate the demands of these parties to keep the coalition intact.

5. The Challenges of Coalition Politics

While coalition politics in India ensures broader representation and inclusivity, it also brings with it a set of unique challenges:

Policy Compromises: One of the biggest challenges in coalition governments is the need to accommodate different, often conflicting, political ideologies. Parties in a coalition may have diverging views on economic, social, and foreign policy, making it difficult to create a coherent and consistent agenda. This can lead to **policy paralysis**, where important decisions are delayed or watered down to avoid conflicts within the coalition.

Instability: Coalitions are inherently fragile, and there is always the risk of internal dissent. Smaller parties within the coalition can exert disproportionate influence, sometimes threatening to withdraw support if their demands are not met. This can lead to **political instability** and frequent changes in government. The 1990s saw a period of unstable coalitions, with multiple general elections taking place in quick succession.

Inefficiency: Coalition governments often focus more on managing internal relationships than on effective governance. With each party trying to assert its priorities, governance can become inefficient, and long-term planning may take a back seat.

Fragmentation of Mandates: In some cases, coalitions can lead to a **fragmented mandate**, where the government's ability to execute its agenda is compromised by the need to cater to too many parties and their regional or factional interests.

6. The Benefits of Coalition Politics

Despite its challenges, coalition politics has also brought several benefits to Indian democracy:

Inclusivity and Representation: Coalition politics ensures that a broader spectrum of the population is represented in the government. Regional parties bring local issues to the national stage, ensuring that governance reflects the diversity of India's population. This inclusivity helps in creating policies that cater to the needs of various communities and regions, leading to more balanced development.

Moderation of Extremism: Coalitions often force parties to moderate their more extreme positions in order to work with others. For example, a party with strong views on a particular issue may have to compromise to gain support from its coalition partners. This ensures that governance is more moderate and less ideologically rigid, which can lead to more pragmatic decision-making.

Checks on Power: Coalition politics can act as a check on **centralized authority**. When a single party holds too much power, it can lead to **authoritarianism** and unchecked decisions. In a coalition, the need to gain the support of multiple parties can prevent any one party from becoming too dominant, thereby fostering **democratic accountability**.

7. Coalition Politics in Modern India

In recent years, India has seen both the strengths and weaknesses of coalition politics. The **United Progressive Alliance (UPA)**, led by the Congress Party, governed from 2004 to 2014 as a coalition of several parties. While the UPA government successfully passed major reforms, it was also plagued by allegations of **corruption** and policy deadlock due to the competing interests of coalition partners.

In contrast, the **National Democratic Alliance (NDA)**, led by the **Bharatiya Janata Party (BJP)** under Prime Minister **Narendra Modi**, has largely governed with a more stable coalition. The BJP's ability to secure a clear majority in the **2014** and **2019** elections has reduced its dependence on smaller coalition partners, allowing it to pursue a more assertive policy agenda. However, the BJP still maintains alliances with regional parties to secure influence in key states.

8. The Future of Coalition Politics in India

The future of coalition politics in India will likely be shaped by the continued fragmentation of the electorate, the rise of regional powers, and the increasing use of **social media** and **technology** in political campaigns. While national parties like the BJP and Congress will remain significant, they will continue to rely on coalitions to govern, especially in states where regional identities and issues dominate the political discourse.

Coalition politics will also continue to be a balancing act between governance and maintaining internal unity. As India's democracy evolves, the ability of political parties to form and manage coalitions effectively will be crucial for the country's political stability and development.

In Summary, coalition politics reflects the **spirit of compromise** and **pluralism** that is at the heart of India's democracy. While coalitions may be challenging to manage, they also provide a platform for diverse voices to be heard and for different interests to be represented. As India's political landscape continues to evolve, coalition politics will remain an integral part of the nation's governance structure, ensuring that democracy in India remains inclusive, dynamic, and representative of its core values.

Party Funding and Campaigns: How Political Campaigns Are Financed

The financing of political parties and campaigns is a critical aspect of the electoral process in any democracy, including India. The way political parties fund their campaigns not only influences the electoral outcomes but also affects the overall health of democracy. In India, the funding of political parties has evolved over the years, shaped by legal frameworks, political dynamics, and the increasing role of money in politics.

1. The Importance of Campaign Financing

Campaign financing is essential for various reasons:

Visibility and Outreach: Political campaigns require substantial funding to create visibility among voters. Parties need to promote their ideologies, manifestos, and candidates through advertisements, rallies, and public engagements. The extent of a party's outreach often correlates with its financial resources.

Logistics and Operations: Running a successful campaign involves extensive logistical operations, including organizing rallies, mobilizing volunteers, and distributing campaign materials. These activities incur significant costs that need to be covered.

Media Engagement: In the age of digital and traditional media, engaging with media outlets to secure coverage is vital. This may involve buying advertising slots on television, newspapers, and social media platforms, all of which require funding.

Voter Engagement: Engaging with voters through door-to-door canvassing, community events, and public forums necessitates resources to mobilize volunteers and staff, further increasing the need for financial backing.

2. Sources of Funding for Political Parties

Political parties in India secure funding from various sources, both formal and informal. Understanding these sources is crucial for analyzing the dynamics of political financing.

Donations from Individuals and Corporations: One of the primary sources of funding for political parties comes from donations made by individuals and corporations. Wealthy individuals or business entities often contribute large sums to political parties in the hope of influencing policy decisions or gaining favorable conditions for their businesses. While this practice is legal, it raises questions about the potential for corruption and the influence of money on policy-making.

Party Membership Fees: Political parties also collect funds through membership fees from their registered members. Although this source of funding is generally smaller compared to corporate donations, it provides parties with a sense of ownership among their base and can help in sustaining grassroots operations.

Government Funding: To promote transparency and reduce corruption, the Indian government has provisions for state funding of political parties. This funding is typically allocated based on the party's performance in previous elections. While government funding exists, the amount is often insufficient to cover the high costs of campaigning, leading parties to seek additional funding sources.

Crowdfunding: With the rise of digital platforms, some political parties have begun to explore crowdfunding as a means of raising campaign funds. This approach allows them to solicit small donations from a large number of supporters, thus reducing dependency on big donors. However, this method is still in its infancy in India and has not yet reached its full potential.

Political Action Committees (PACs): While not as prevalent in India as in some other democracies, political action committees may emerge in the future. These organizations can collect contributions to fund specific candidates or initiatives and are typically associated with specific interest groups or sectors.

3. Legal Framework for Campaign Financing in India

India has a set of laws and regulations governing political party funding to promote transparency and accountability:

Representation of the People Act, 1951: This Act lays the foundation for the regulation of political party funding. It mandates that political parties must maintain accounts and submit annual reports to the Election Commission of India. However, enforcement remains a challenge, and many parties do not adhere strictly to these regulations.

Electoral Bonds: Introduced in 2018, electoral bonds are a financial instrument that allows individuals and corporations to donate to political parties without disclosing their identity. While this system was designed to promote anonymous funding and encourage donations, critics argue that it undermines transparency and allows for unlimited and unaccountable corporate influence in politics.

Income Tax Exemptions: Political parties in India can receive tax exemptions on donations received. Section 80GGC of the Income Tax Act allows individuals making contributions to political parties to claim deductions on their taxable income, further incentivizing donations.

4. The Impact of Money in Politics

The financing of political campaigns has significant implications for the functioning of democracy in India:

Corruption and Influence: The infusion of large sums of money into politics often leads to corruption, as parties may become beholden to their donors, influencing their policy decisions. This can create a situation where the interests of the wealthy override the needs of the general populace, undermining democratic principles.

Disparity Between Parties: Parties with access to significant financial resources can dominate the electoral landscape, making it challenging for smaller or regional parties to compete effectively. This disparity can lead to a lack of diversity in political representation and limit voter choice.

Public Trust and Perception: The perception of money's influence in politics can erode public trust in political institutions. When citizens believe that elections are won by those who can spend the most, it diminishes faith in the democratic process and leads to disillusionment with governance.

5. The Role of Civil Society and Media

Civil society organizations and the media play a crucial role in monitoring and advocating for transparent campaign financing:

Advocacy for Reform: Civil society organizations have long been advocating for reforms in campaign financing to enhance transparency and accountability. Their efforts often focus on limiting corporate donations, promoting public funding, and ensuring strict enforcement of existing laws.

Investigative Journalism: Investigative journalists have been instrumental in exposing corruption and malpractice related to campaign financing. Their reports shed light on the intricate relationships between politicians and donors, helping to hold parties accountable for their funding sources.

The Future of Political Funding in India

As India continues to evolve as a democracy, the financing of political parties and campaigns will remain a contentious issue. Ensuring transparency and accountability in campaign financing is crucial for the health of Indian democracy. As the public becomes more aware of the implications of money in politics, there is a growing demand for reforms that promote ethical fundraising practices and reduce the influence of money in decision-making.

The future of political funding in India will likely hinge on a balance between enabling parties to effectively compete in elections and safeguarding against corruption and undue influence. The role of citizens in demanding accountability, along with the efforts of civil society and the media, will be vital in shaping a more transparent and equitable political financing system in the years to come.

A Quick Comparison with Political Parties in Other Democracies

Political parties are fundamental to the functioning of democracies around the world. While the concept of political parties exists globally, their structures, funding mechanisms, and electoral strategies vary significantly from one country to another. This section aims to provide a comparative analysis of political parties in India with those in other democracies, focusing on party systems, funding, and the relationship between parties and voters.

1. Types of Party Systems

Political parties can be categorized based on the number of parties that participate in the political process. The most common systems are single-party systems, two-party systems, and multi-party systems.

- **Single-Party Systems**: In some countries, such as China and North Korea, a single party monopolizes political power. For instance, the Communist Party of China controls the political landscape, with no legal opposition. In such systems, political parties serve more as vehicles for the ruling party's agenda rather than functioning as platforms for democratic debate and competition.
- **Two-Party Systems**: Countries like the United States and the United Kingdom operate under two-party systems, where two dominant parties primarily compete for power. In the U.S.,

the Democratic and Republican parties have historically alternated in governance, often leading to stable but polarized political landscapes. The two-party system can limit voter choice, as smaller parties often struggle to gain traction due to systemic barriers, such as the "winner-takes-all" electoral system.

- **Multi-Party Systems**: India is classified as a multi-party system, characterized by the existence of numerous political parties vying for power at national and regional levels. This diversity allows for a wider range of political representation, accommodating various interests and identities within the population. However, it can also lead to fragmented mandates, necessitating coalition governments, which may complicate governance.

2. Party Funding and Financial Transparency

The funding mechanisms for political parties vary significantly between India and other democracies, impacting their operations and accountability.

- **India**: Political parties in India rely on a mix of public funding, individual donations, and corporate contributions. The introduction of electoral bonds aimed to increase donations while maintaining donor anonymity, but this has raised concerns over transparency and potential corruption. While parties are required to disclose funding sources, compliance is often lacking, making it difficult to assess the true nature of party financing.

- **United States**: In contrast, the U.S. political funding system is heavily influenced by the Supreme Court's decision in *Citizens United v. FEC* (2010), which allowed corporations and unions to spend unlimited amounts on independent political expenditures. This has led to significant financial power being concentrated in the hands of a few wealthy donors and Political Action Committees (PACs), which can greatly influence elections and policy decisions. The lack of transparency in campaign financing has led to widespread public concern about the role of money in politics.

- **Germany**: Germany's political financing system includes state funding for political parties based on their electoral performance. This approach aims to reduce dependency on large donors and enhance democratic accountability. Parties must adhere to strict rules regarding campaign financing, and any violations can result in penalties. The emphasis on transparency is designed to foster public trust in the political system.

3. Party-Voter Relationship

The relationship between political parties and voters varies widely across democracies, influencing how parties approach governance and accountability.

- **India**: In India, the connection between parties and voters is often shaped by identity politics, regional affiliations, and personal charisma of leaders. Political parties frequently mobilize support based on caste, religion, or regional identity, which can lead to transactional politics, where voters may prioritize immediate benefits over long-term governance. The loyalty to parties can be deeply rooted in historical and cultural contexts, but there is also a growing demand for accountability and transparency among younger voters.
- **Scandinavia**: In contrast, Scandinavian countries like Sweden and Denmark exhibit a different dynamic. Political parties in these nations often maintain strong ties with civil society organizations and trade unions, fostering a collaborative approach to policymaking. Voter engagement tends to be higher, with parties focusing on substantive issues such as welfare, education, and health care rather than identity politics. This results in a more issue-oriented political discourse, enhancing accountability and responsiveness to citizens' needs.

- **Latin America**: Many Latin American countries have experienced volatile party-voter relationships, marked by shifting allegiances and the rise of populist movements. Leaders like Hugo Chávez in Venezuela and Evo Morales in Bolivia capitalized on widespread discontent with traditional political parties, often positioning themselves as representatives of the marginalized. This shift highlights the impact of socio-economic conditions on party dynamics, where voters may turn to alternative parties or movements that promise radical change.

Learning from Global Examples

The comparison of political parties in India with those in other democracies reveals both challenges and opportunities. While India's multi-party system allows for diverse representation, issues of funding transparency and the influence of identity politics complicate the political landscape. By examining the successes and failures of political party systems worldwide, Indian political stakeholders can identify best practices and adapt strategies that enhance democratic accountability, voter engagement, and effective governance.

As democracy continues to evolve, the interplay between political parties, voters, and the broader political context will remain crucial. A deeper understanding of these dynamics can pave the way for more robust political parties that truly represent the interests of the people and contribute positively to the democratic process.

Conclusion

The landscape of political parties in India is a dynamic and multifaceted arena that reflects the complexities of the nation itself. This chapter has explored the rise and evolution of political parties, the intricacies of coalition politics, and the mechanisms of party funding and campaigning, illustrating how these elements are interconnected in shaping the political fabric of the country.

1. Importance of Political Parties in a Democracy

Political parties play a critical role in a democracy, serving as a bridge between the electorate and the government. They organize political representation, articulate diverse interests, and provide voters with choices. In India, where societal diversity is vast, political parties reflect various identities, aspirations, and regional concerns. This representation is essential for the healthy functioning of democracy, ensuring that different voices are heard and considered in the policy-making process.

2. Evolution and Adaptation

The evolution of political parties in India has been marked by significant historical milestones and social transformations. From the Indian National Congress (INC) leading the struggle for independence to the emergence of regional parties and the Bharatiya Janata Party (BJP) consolidating its position as a major political force, the trajectory of political parties illustrates a response to changing societal needs and aspirations. Parties have had to adapt to the changing political landscape, often recalibrating their ideologies and strategies to resonate with the electorate.

This adaptability is particularly evident in the context of coalition politics, which has become a hallmark of Indian governance. As single-party dominance wanes, the necessity for alliances and coalitions to form stable governments has led to the rise of regional parties and interest-based coalitions. This fragmentation of the political landscape presents both challenges and opportunities, as it encourages negotiation and consensus-building while complicating governance.

3. The Challenge of Corruption and Funding

However, the relationship between political parties and the electorate is not without its challenges. Issues of corruption and the opaque nature of party funding have raised concerns about accountability and transparency in the political process. The reliance on corporate donations and the potential for black money to influence politics threaten the integrity of the democratic system. These challenges underscore the need for reforms in party funding and campaign finance to ensure that political parties remain accountable to the public and that the interests of ordinary citizens are prioritized over those of a select few.

4. Looking Ahead: The Future of Political Parties in India

As India moves forward, the future of political parties will depend on their ability to engage with an increasingly informed and active electorate. The rise of social media and digital platforms has transformed how parties communicate with voters, allowing for greater engagement and mobilization. This shift presents an opportunity for parties to connect with younger voters who are seeking authenticity, transparency, and relevance in political discourse.

Furthermore, the evolution of political parties must align with the broader goals of governance, development, and social justice. Parties that prioritize inclusive policies, uphold democratic values, and respond to the needs of marginalized communities are likely to garner greater support in an increasingly competitive political environment.

A Call for Responsible Politics

In conclusion, political parties are indispensable to the democratic process in India. They serve as vehicles for political expression, advocacy, and governance. However, to fulfill their role effectively, parties must navigate the complexities of a diverse society while addressing pressing issues such as corruption, funding transparency, and voter engagement.

The onus is on political parties to demonstrate accountability and integrity in their operations, fostering a political culture that encourages participation and trust among citizens. As India continues to evolve as a democracy, the responsible behavior of political parties will be paramount in shaping the nation's political future and ensuring that the ideals of democracy are realized for all its citizens.

PART II: CORRUPTION AND ITS IMPACT

| 5 |

The Roots of Corruption in India

Corruption is often regarded as one of the most significant challenges facing India today, affecting everything from economic growth to social equality. Its roots run deep in Indian society, impacting almost every institution, from the political system to the bureaucracy. This chapter delves into the origins of corruption, its various forms, and provides an unbiased exploration of key corruption scandals across different political eras, highlighting how no party or government has remained untouched by the issue.

Historical Overview: The Colonial Influence on Corruption in India

1. Introduction to Colonial Corruption

Corruption has deep historical roots in India, particularly influenced by the colonial rule that lasted for nearly two centuries. The British colonial administration instituted a complex system of governance that not only exploited India's resources but also fostered a culture of corruption that has persisted through the years. This historical overview seeks to illuminate the foundational aspects of corruption during the colonial era and how these legacies continue to influence contemporary Indian politics and governance.

2. The Nature of Colonial Governance

The British colonial administration in India was characterized by a centralized and bureaucratic system that sought to exert control over vast territories and diverse populations. To manage this complex landscape, the British implemented a hierarchical structure that often sidelined local governance and traditional systems. The British employed a combination of coercive measures and bureaucratic inefficiencies that bred corruption at multiple levels of administration.

- **Bureaucratic Structure and Patronage** The colonial bureaucracy was primarily staffed by British officials who were not always accountable to the Indian populace. This lack of accountability, combined with a patronage system that rewarded loyalty over competence, created an environment ripe for corruption. Indian officials, often caught between colonial mandates and local pressures, resorted to corrupt practices as a means of survival and advancement within the bureaucratic hierarchy.
- **The "Divide and Rule" Policy** The British also employed a "divide and rule" strategy, exacerbating existing social and communal divisions within Indian society. This tactic not only facilitated control but also encouraged corrupt practices as various groups competed for power and favor from the colonial authorities. By playing different communities against one another, the British undermined the collective power of the Indian populace, making it easier for corruption to thrive.

3. The Role of Economic Exploitation

The economic policies of the British Empire significantly contributed to the culture of corruption. The British focused on extracting resources from India, often at the expense of local welfare. The forced cultivation of cash crops, such as cotton and indigo, prioritized profit over the needs of the local population, leading to widespread poverty and disenfranchisement. This economic exploitation fueled corruption as local officials sought bribes or kickbacks to circumvent colonial regulations or secure favorable treatment for local communities.

- **Revenue Collection and Corruption** The system of revenue collection became a notorious area of corruption. The British imposed taxes on land and agricultural produce, often leading to oppressive burdens on farmers. Local revenue collectors, driven by quotas and the need to meet targets, often resorted to corrupt practices such as extortion or falsifying records to inflate tax revenues. These practices not only drained resources from the local economy but also alienated the agrarian population, sowing distrust in the administrative framework.

4. Institutionalizing Corruption

The colonial government inadvertently institutionalized corruption through a lack of transparency and accountability. Laws and regulations were often vague, leading to arbitrary enforcement and opportunities for bribery. The colonial judiciary was similarly corrupt, where justice could be bought, and legal outcomes often favored the wealthy and influential.

- **The Legal Framework** The legal system established during colonial rule was designed to serve the interests of the British, and its complexities were often exploited by those with resources to manipulate outcomes. This legal environment fostered a culture where corruption was normalized as a means of navigating the bureaucratic maze.

5. Post-Independence Legacy

The legacy of colonial corruption has had lasting effects on post-independence India. Upon gaining independence in 1947, India inherited a bureaucratic structure riddled with inefficiencies and corrupt practices. Many of the systemic issues, such as lack of accountability and transparency, continued to plague governance, making it difficult to uproot the deep-seated culture of corruption.

- **Continuity of Practices** The political landscape of independent India saw the emergence of political parties that often mimicked the corrupt practices of their colonial predecessors. The patronage networks that flourished during colonial rule found new life in post-independence politics, as political leaders and bureaucrats engaged in corrupt practices for personal gain, often prioritizing loyalty over merit.

Understanding the Roots of Corruption

In conclusion, the colonial influence on corruption in India has created a complex tapestry of governance challenges that persist to this day. Understanding this historical context is crucial for comprehending the evolution of corruption in India. As the nation continues to grapple with issues of transparency, accountability, and governance, recognizing the deep-seated roots of corruption can provide valuable insights for creating effective reforms and promoting ethical governance in the future.

By addressing the historical foundations of corruption, India can better navigate its contemporary challenges and work toward a more accountable and transparent political system that serves the needs of all its citizens.

Types of Corruption: From Bureaucratic to Political Corruption

Corruption in India manifests in various forms, affecting multiple levels of governance and impacting the daily lives of citizens. Understanding the different types of corruption is crucial for diagnosing the problems within the political and bureaucratic systems, as well as for crafting effective anti-corruption strategies. This section categorizes corruption into bureaucratic corruption, political corruption, and other forms, examining their characteristics, implications, and examples.

1. Bureaucratic Corruption

Bureaucratic corruption, also known as administrative corruption, occurs within the public sector, where government officials exploit their positions for personal gain. This form of corruption is particularly detrimental as it erodes public trust in institutions and affects service delivery to citizens.

- **Bribery** One of the most common forms of bureaucratic corruption is bribery, where individuals or businesses pay officials to secure favorable treatment, permits, or licenses. For instance, citizens may offer bribes to police officers for avoiding fines or to government clerks for expediting paperwork. This creates a vicious cycle where ordinary citizens feel compelled to engage in corrupt practices to obtain basic services.
- **Embezzlement** Embezzlement involves the misappropriation of funds entrusted to an official's care. In many cases, public servants may siphon off government funds meant for public projects, such as infrastructure development or social welfare schemes. This not only affects the quality of services provided to citizens but also diverts resources from critical areas of need.
- **Nepotism and Favoritism** Bureaucratic corruption also manifests through nepotism and favoritism, where officials grant jobs, contracts, or benefits to family members, friends, or associates, regardless of their qualifications. This practice compromises meritocracy in the public sector and leads to inefficiencies and disillusionment among qualified candidates who may be overlooked.

2. Political Corruption

Political corruption refers to unethical behavior by politicians and public officials that involves the misuse of power for personal or party gain. This form of corruption can undermine democratic processes and lead to a lack of accountability in governance.

- **Electoral Corruption** Electoral corruption is a pervasive issue in Indian politics, manifesting through practices such as vote-buying, manipulation of voter rolls, and the use of muscle power to intimidate voters. Political parties may offer money, gifts, or other incentives to secure votes, particularly in high-stakes elections. This compromises the integrity of the electoral process and erodes public confidence in democracy.
- **Corruption in Governance** Political leaders may engage in corrupt practices while in office, using their authority to award contracts to favored businesses or divert public funds for personal use. The allocation of government contracts to companies owned by party members or affiliates is a common example of this form of corruption. Such actions not only perpetuate a culture of corruption but also impact public policy, often prioritizing the interests of a few over the welfare of the general populace.
- **Policy Manipulation** Political corruption can also occur through the manipulation of policies for personal gain. For example, politicians may introduce or amend laws that favor their business interests or those of their allies. This form of corruption has severe consequences for governance, as it can lead to policies that benefit a select few rather than addressing the needs of the broader society.

3. Other Forms of Corruption

In addition to bureaucratic and political corruption, several other forms of corruption exist, each with unique characteristics and implications for society.

- **Corporate Corruption** Corporate corruption involves unethical practices by businesses, such as bribing government officials to secure contracts or favorable regulations. This can create a toxic environment where business decisions are driven by corruption rather than competition or innovation, ultimately harming consumers and stifling economic growth.

- **Media Corruption** Media corruption occurs when journalists or media organizations engage in unethical practices, such as accepting bribes to suppress stories or promote biased reporting. This compromises the role of the media as a watchdog and can distort public perceptions of issues, affecting political accountability.

- **Social Corruption** Social corruption includes practices that exploit social vulnerabilities, such as trafficking, exploitation of labor, and corruption in the delivery of social services. This form of corruption often targets marginalized communities, exacerbating inequalities and hindering social progress.

4. Implications of Corruption

Understanding the various types of corruption is essential for recognizing their implications on society and governance. Corruption undermines public trust in institutions, leads to inefficient use of resources, and stifles economic development. It also contributes to social inequalities, as those with power and resources can manipulate systems to their advantage, further marginalizing vulnerable populations.

In conclusion, the types of corruption in India—ranging from bureaucratic to political, corporate, and social—highlight the multifaceted nature of the problem. Addressing these different forms requires comprehensive strategies that promote transparency, accountability, and ethical governance. By understanding the various manifestations of corruption, citizens, policymakers, and reform advocates can work towards creating a more equitable and just society, rooted in integrity and public service.

Case Studies of Landmark Corruption Scandals

Corruption scandals in India have significantly shaped the political landscape and public perception of governance. This section delves into some of the most notorious cases, illustrating how they have not only exposed the vulnerabilities within the system but also ignited public outrage and calls for reform. We will cover landmark scandals, including both historical and recent events, to provide a comprehensive overview of corruption's impact on Indian society.

1. The Bofors Scandal (1980s)

One of India's earliest high-profile corruption scandals, the Bofors case involved allegations of kickbacks in a ⬦1,437 crore ($210 million) artillery gun deal with a Swedish company, Bofors AB. The scandal broke in 1987 when reports emerged that a substantial portion of the contract amount had been siphoned off as bribes to Indian officials, including prominent politicians.

Impact:

The Bofors scandal significantly impacted the political career of then-Prime Minister Rajiv Gandhi, leading to his eventual defeat in the 1989 general elections. It underscored the need for greater transparency in defense procurement and led to public skepticism towards political leadership.

2. The 2G Spectrum Scam (2008)

The 2G Spectrum Scam is one of the largest corruption scandals in India's history, involving the allocation of telecom licenses and spectrum in 2008. The Comptroller and Auditor General (CAG) reported a potential loss to the exchequer of ⬦1.76 lakh crore ($26 billion) due to irregularities in the auction process. Key figures, including then-Communications Minister A. Raja, were accused of favoring certain companies, allegedly receiving kickbacks in return.

Impact:

The fallout from the 2G scandal was monumental, leading to numerous arrests and a prolonged legal battle. It sparked widespread protests and heightened public awareness regarding corruption in telecommunications and public service.

3. Commonwealth Games Scam (2010)

The Commonwealth Games held in Delhi were marred by allegations of widespread corruption, mismanagement, and financial irregularities. The estimated loss to the public exchequer was around ₹70,000 crore ($10 billion) due to inflated contracts, kickbacks, and inadequate oversight of funds.

Impact:

The scandal drew national and international criticism, leading to a tarnished image of India on the global stage. Investigations revealed a nexus between government officials and contractors, prompting calls for accountability and reform in the management of large-scale events.

4. The Adarsh Housing Society Scam (2010)

This scandal involved the illegal allocation of prime land meant for war widows and veterans in Mumbai to a housing society, which included politicians, bureaucrats, and military officials as members. The scam raised questions about the misuse of authority and the erosion of ethical standards in governance.

Impact:

The Adarsh Housing Society Scam led to significant political fallout, resulting in the resignation of several officials and calls for stricter regulations regarding land use and allocation.

5. The Vyapam Scam (2010-2015)

The Vyapam (Vyavasayik Pariksha Mandal) scam revolved around a massive examination and recruitment racket in Madhya Pradesh, where politicians, bureaucrats, and businessmen colluded to facilitate cheating in various exams. The scandal involved bribery, impersonation, and even mysterious deaths of key witnesses.

Impact:

The Vyapam scam sparked nationwide outrage, revealing the deep-rooted corruption in the education and recruitment systems. It prompted investigations that led to the arrest of numerous officials and raised significant concerns about the integrity of public examinations.

6. The Punjab National Bank (PNB) Fraud (2018)

The PNB fraud involved a ₹14,000 crore ($2.2 billion) scam orchestrated by billionaire jeweler Nirav Modi and his uncle Mehul Choksi. They allegedly obtained fraudulent letters of undertaking from the bank, which facilitated loans from other banks without adequate collateral.

Impact:

The PNB scam led to a loss of confidence in the banking system and exposed vulnerabilities in regulatory mechanisms. It also prompted calls for banking reforms and stricter oversight of financial institutions.

7. The Satyendar Jain Case (2022)

Delhi's Health Minister, Satyendar Jain, faced allegations of money laundering and corruption linked to his businesses prior to entering politics. Investigations by the Enforcement Directorate (ED) revealed discrepancies in his financial dealings, prompting significant media attention and public discourse.

Impact:

The Jain case has intensified discussions around corruption in local governance and the accountability of public officials, reflecting ongoing challenges in combating corruption at various levels of government.

8. The Maharashtra Political Crisis and Allegations (2022)

The political upheaval in Maharashtra, culminating in the collapse of the Uddhav Thackeray-led government, brought to light various corruption allegations against leaders from different political parties. Accusations ranged from bribery in land deals to misuse of government funds, leading to an intensified scrutiny of political alliances.

Impact:

This crisis has highlighted the complexities of coalition politics in India and raised questions about the accountability of elected representatives. The public's reaction underscored a growing demand for transparency in governance.

9. The Punjab and Haryana High Court Decision on Political Funding (2023)

In a recent judgment, the Punjab and Haryana High Court ruled on the need for greater transparency in political funding, calling for stricter regulations on party donations and accountability. This decision reflects growing concern over the influence of money in politics and the necessity for reform.

Impact:

The ruling has reignited debates around electoral reforms and the need for cleaner politics in India. It emphasizes the public's desire for a system where political financing is transparent and ethical.

The case studies of landmark corruption scandals in India illustrate the pervasive nature of corruption across various sectors and levels of government. Each scandal has not only exposed the vulnerabilities within the political system but also spurred public outrage, mobilizing citizens to demand accountability and reform. These events serve as a reminder of the critical importance of transparency, integrity, and active civic engagement in combating corruption and fostering a healthier democracy. As India continues to evolve, addressing the roots and ramifications of corruption will be paramount in building a just and equitable society for all citizens.

Conclusion

The roots of corruption in India are deep, stretching back to the colonial period and continuing to plague the country even after independence. Corruption has evolved from bureaucratic bribery to large-scale political scandals, with each case damaging the public's trust in democratic institutions. Despite multiple landmark scandals implicating governments from across the political spectrum, comprehensive reforms have been slow to materialize.

Understanding the history and types of corruption, along with its devastating effects on society, is crucial to combating it effectively. The responsibility lies not only with the government but also with civil society, the media, and the general public to demand greater transparency, accountability, and reforms to reduce the impact of corruption on India's growth and development.

In addition to the verified scams, India's political landscape has also seen numerous alleged or viral corruption cases that, although yet to be fully substantiated or proven in courts, have captured public attention and become part of political discourse. These cases often spread quickly through media, creating a perception of corruption even in instances where legal proceedings are ongoing or inconclusive. Here's a brief look at some of the most talked-about controversies that have gained traction among the public:

1. Rafale Deal Controversy

- **What happened**: The **Rafale fighter jet deal** between India and France became a major point of political debate and controversy, with allegations that the Indian government under **Prime Minister Narendra Modi** had overpaid for the jets and provided undue favors to industrialists.
- **Viral Status**: Though the deal was cleared by the **Supreme Court of India** in 2019, public discourse continues, fueled by opposition parties like the Congress, which alleged that the government bypassed proper procurement procedures.
- **Outcome**: Despite several investigations, no conclusive evidence of wrongdoing has been found, but the controversy remains a point of contention in political debates.

2. Adani Group Controversy

- **What happened**: The **Adani Group**, led by industrialist **Gautam Adani**, has faced multiple allegations, including accusations of benefiting from crony capitalism and securing favorable contracts and loans due to its close proximity to the government. Allegations also surfaced about the rapid rise of the group's wealth.

- **Viral Status**: The Adani Group's rapid expansion in sectors like infrastructure, energy, and ports has raised questions among opposition parties, with allegations of government favoritism. However, the group has consistently denied these claims, and no concrete evidence has emerged.
- **Outcome**: Investigations into the Adani Group's finances are ongoing, but public sentiment around its close association with the government remains divided.

3. Pegasus Spyware Allegations

- **What happened**: In 2021, reports surfaced that several Indian politicians, journalists, and activists had been targeted using **Pegasus spyware**, allegedly by government agencies. This sparked outrage, with accusations that the government was engaging in illegal surveillance.
- **Viral Status**: The Pegasus scandal went viral, becoming a massive point of political debate, especially since it allegedly involved spying on opposition leaders and activists. The government has denied any wrongdoing, but the matter continues to be a hot-button issue.
- **Outcome**: Investigations are still underway, but no definitive proof has been presented. The issue remains unresolved and is often highlighted as an example of alleged government overreach.

4. Alleged COVID-19 Relief Fund Mismanagement (PM CARES Fund)

- **What happened**: The **PM CARES Fund**, set up during the COVID-19 pandemic for relief efforts, has been a subject of intense public scrutiny. Opposition leaders and critics raised concerns about the transparency and accountability of the fund, questioning how donations were used.

- **Viral Status**: The lack of clear public disclosure about the fund's finances led to viral speculation that the fund was being misused. Despite repeated calls for greater transparency, the fund's details remain mostly private.
- **Outcome**: The government has maintained that the fund was used appropriately, but calls for independent audits and greater transparency continue.

5. Sushant Singh Rajput Death and Alleged Drug Nexus

- **What happened**: The tragic death of actor **Sushant Singh Rajput** in 2020 led to widespread speculation about foul play, with allegations that Bollywood celebrities, politicians, and big business houses were part of an extensive drug nexus.
- **Viral Status**: While no direct evidence linked political figures to the case, the viral nature of the allegations stirred debates about corruption in Bollywood and its ties with powerful political figures.
- **Outcome**: Investigations by multiple agencies, including the **CBI** and **Narcotics Control Bureau (NCB)**, did not conclusively prove the involvement of political figures, but the case remains fresh in public memory due to its viral coverage.

6. Vyapam Scam Deaths and Conspiracy

- **What happened**: The **Vyapam scam**, as mentioned earlier, involved a recruitment and admission fraud in Madhya Pradesh. What made this case even more notorious was the series of mysterious deaths connected to individuals involved in the investigation.
- **Viral Status**: The sudden and unexplained deaths of witnesses, accused individuals, and journalists involved in the investigation led to viral theories about a larger conspiracy, involving influential politicians and bureaucrats.

- **Outcome**: Despite multiple arrests and convictions, questions about the full extent of the scam remain, and the deaths associated with it continue to fuel public speculation.

7. Alleged Land Scams

- **What happened**: Several state governments across India, including in Maharashtra, Uttar Pradesh, and Haryana, have faced allegations of **land acquisition scandals**, where politicians were accused of misusing their powers to buy land at undervalued prices and sell them at exorbitant rates.
- **Viral Status**: Land scams have always been a hot topic of debate in India, especially given the rapid urbanization of cities. These allegations often go viral, with accusations of politicians amassing large land banks under dubious circumstances.
- **Outcome**: In many cases, investigations have been launched, but conclusive action has often been slow. Land scams continue to be a significant issue in political discourse.

8. Mining Scams

- **What happened**: Illegal mining operations, particularly in states like **Goa, Karnataka**, and **Odisha**, have been another point of contention. Politicians and businesspeople were accused of illegal extraction of natural resources, leading to significant environmental damage and loss of revenue to the state.
- **Viral Status**: Mining scams have been a recurring viral topic, with many opposition parties accusing ruling governments of turning a blind eye to illegal operations in exchange for bribes.
- **Outcome**: Some high-profile arrests have been made, but illegal mining continues to be a concern in these states.

While many of these cases remain speculative or unproven, they highlight a larger issue in Indian politics: the public perception of widespread corruption. Whether or not these allegations are proven in court, they influence how the electorate views politicians, parties, and the overall system.

Corruption scandals and viral allegations are symptomatic of a deeper malaise in Indian governance, where the lack of transparency, slow judicial processes, and political opportunism create an environment ripe for suspicion and conspiracy theories. For young readers, these cases provide a lens through which to view the importance of vigilance, civic engagement, and demand for greater accountability from political leaders.

In a world driven by information and digital platforms, where news spreads like wildfire, it's crucial for the youth to approach such cases with an analytical mind, discerning between factual evidence and speculation, while striving for a more transparent and accountable system of governance.

| 6 |

Corruption in Indian Politics Today

Corruption remains one of the most persistent issues in Indian politics, shaping governance, public services, and even the daily lives of citizens. In this chapter, we'll explore how political corruption manifests in the modern landscape, how it affects both governance and the common people, and the critical role of the judiciary in controlling or sometimes facilitating this phenomenon. The focus will remain unbiased, highlighting that corruption is not a one-party problem but a systemic issue affecting all political actors across the board.

Political Corruption: A Systemic Issue

Political corruption is a pervasive and systemic problem that undermines the very foundations of democracy and governance in India. It manifests in various forms and affects all levels of government, creating a complex web of practices that can inhibit effective policy-making and equitable resource distribution. To understand the depth and breadth of political corruption in India today, it is essential to explore its causes, implications, and the multifaceted dimensions that characterize this pressing issue.

Understanding Political Corruption

At its core, political corruption refers to the abuse of power by government officials for personal gain. This includes a range of illicit activities, such as bribery, embezzlement, nepotism, and influence peddling. Unlike other forms of corruption, which may be confined to bureaucratic or business environments, political corruption specifically involves elected officials and political leaders who wield significant power over public policy and resource allocation.

In India, political corruption is often intertwined with the broader socio-economic landscape, where poverty, inequality, and lack of access to basic services create fertile ground for corrupt practices. Politicians may resort to corruption as a means to maintain their power, secure funding for campaigns, or fulfill personal financial interests.

Causes of Political Corruption

Several factors contribute to the prevalence of political corruption in India:

1. **Weak Institutional Frameworks**: The effectiveness of institutions designed to combat corruption, such as anti-corruption agencies and judicial bodies, is often compromised by political interference, lack of resources, and bureaucratic inefficiencies. This creates an environment where corrupt practices can thrive without fear of accountability.

2. **Lack of Transparency**: The opacity of political processes and decision-making contributes significantly to corruption. When government actions are not subject to scrutiny, there is little incentive for officials to act ethically. The absence of transparency in political funding, government contracts, and public procurement can lead to widespread corruption.

3. **Cultural Tolerance for Corruption**: In many cases, there exists a societal acceptance or tolerance for corrupt practices, often viewed as a necessary means to navigate bureaucratic obstacles. This cultural normalization of corruption can perpetuate a cycle where individuals believe that engaging in corrupt practices is the only way to succeed or obtain services.

4. **Political Funding**: The financing of political campaigns plays a crucial role in fostering corruption. In the absence of strin-

gent regulations on political funding, candidates often resort to illegal sources of money, which may require them to engage in corrupt practices once they are in power to recoup their investments. This cycle of dependency can lead to a significant distortion of political priorities.

Implications of Political Corruption

The implications of political corruption extend beyond individual acts of malfeasance; they have far-reaching effects on governance, public trust, and societal well-being:

1. **Erosion of Public Trust**: Political corruption undermines citizens' trust in government institutions and elected officials. When corruption becomes pervasive, public faith in democracy is compromised, leading to cynicism and disengagement from the political process.

2. **Inequitable Resource Distribution**: Corruption often skews resource allocation in favor of the politically connected, marginalizing those without power. This leads to inequities in access to essential services like education, healthcare, and infrastructure, further entrenching social and economic disparities.

3. **Policy Distortion**: When political decisions are driven by corrupt interests rather than the public good, policies can become ineffective or even harmful. For instance, legislation that favors specific industries or businesses due to bribery can undermine competition, stifle innovation, and lead to poor public outcomes.

4. **Impediments to Development**: Corruption acts as a barrier to sustainable development. Foreign investment is often deterred by the perception of high levels of corruption, limiting opportunities for economic growth and technological advancement.

Addressing Political Corruption

Combating political corruption in India requires a multifaceted approach:

1. **Strengthening Institutions**: Enhancing the independence and efficacy of anti-corruption bodies and judicial systems is crucial for holding corrupt officials accountable. Empowering these institutions with the necessary resources and legal backing will enable them to investigate and prosecute corrupt activities more effectively.

2. **Promoting Transparency and Accountability**: Implementing mechanisms for greater transparency in political funding, government contracts, and public spending can help deter corruption. Initiatives like the Right to Information (RTI) Act should be strengthened to ensure that citizens have access to information regarding governmental decisions and expenditures.

3. **Encouraging Civic Engagement**: Public awareness campaigns and civic education can play a vital role in mobilizing citizens against corruption. Engaging communities in oversight processes and decision-making can empower citizens to demand accountability from their elected representatives.

4. **Reforming Political Financing**: Establishing stricter regulations on political funding and implementing public financing options for campaigns can help reduce the influence of money in politics. This would create a more level playing field for candidates and minimize the temptation to engage in corrupt practices.

Political corruption remains a systemic issue in India, deeply rooted in historical, social, and economic contexts. Addressing it requires a comprehensive understanding of its causes and implications, alongside concerted efforts to reform institutions, promote transparency, and engage citizens in the fight against corruption. By recognizing the challenges posed by political corruption and committing to meaningful reforms, India can work toward a more transparent, accountable, and equitable democratic process that serves the interests of all its citizens.

The Role of the Judiciary in Controlling or Facilitating Corruption

The judiciary serves as a fundamental pillar of democracy, tasked with upholding the rule of law and ensuring justice. In the context of political corruption, the judiciary plays a dual role: it can act as a powerful tool for combating corruption and safeguarding the rights of citizens, or it can, in some cases, become complicit in corrupt practices. Understanding this complex dynamic is crucial for grasping the impact of the judiciary on corruption in India.

Guardians of the Constitution

The judiciary's primary responsibility is to interpret and uphold the Constitution of India. The Constitution enshrines various fundamental rights, including the right to equality, the right to a fair trial, and the right to freedom of speech and expression. By enforcing these rights, the judiciary acts as a check on the abuse of power by both the executive and legislative branches.

Judicial review allows courts to evaluate the constitutionality of laws and government actions. This power is critical in addressing corruption, as it enables the judiciary to strike down laws that may facilitate corrupt practices or infringe upon citizens' rights. For instance, when laws related to political funding or electoral practices are found to be unconstitutional, the judiciary can intervene to prevent further exploitation.

Enforcement of Anti-Corruption Laws

The judiciary is instrumental in enforcing anti-corruption laws, such as the Prevention of Corruption Act, 1988. Through various legal proceedings, courts can hold corrupt officials accountable, impose penalties, and ensure that justice is served. High-profile cases against politicians and bureaucrats have demonstrated the judiciary's ability to act against corruption.

1. **Public Interest Litigation (PIL)**: One significant mechanism through which the judiciary has tackled corruption is the Public Interest Litigation system. PILs allow individuals or groups to file petitions in court on behalf of those unable to do so themselves, thereby facilitating access to justice. This has enabled the judiciary to address systemic issues, including corruption in public services, environmental violations, and social injustices.

2. **Fast-Track Courts**: The establishment of fast-track courts for corruption cases has aimed to expedite the legal process and deliver swift justice. These courts help reduce the backlog of cases and demonstrate the judiciary's commitment to addressing corruption effectively. However, the effectiveness of these courts has often been hampered by procedural delays and the influence of powerful political figures.

Protecting Whistleblowers and Informants

The judiciary also plays a critical role in protecting whistleblowers and informants who expose corruption. Many individuals who come forward to report corrupt practices face threats, harassment, or retribution from powerful actors. Courts can provide protection to whistleblowers, ensuring that their rights are safeguarded and that they can testify without fear of retaliation.

Recent judgments have emphasized the need to protect whistleblowers, recognizing that their disclosures are vital for maintaining transparency and accountability in governance. By providing legal safeguards, the judiciary encourages citizens to participate actively in the fight against corruption.

Challenges and Limitations

Despite its significant role, the judiciary faces numerous challenges in combating political corruption:

1. **Judicial Independence**: The independence of the judiciary is paramount for it to function effectively as a check on corruption. However, political interference, particularly in the appointment and transfer of judges, can compromise judicial impartiality. This can lead to a perception of bias or corruption within the judiciary itself.

2. **Backlog of Cases**: The Indian judicial system is burdened with a massive backlog of cases, leading to significant delays in justice delivery. When corruption cases drag on for years, it undermines the public's faith in the legal system and allows corrupt officials to escape accountability.

3. **Corruption within the Judiciary**: The judiciary is not immune to corruption. Instances of judicial corruption can severely undermine the credibility of the legal system. Ensuring transparency in the functioning of the judiciary, as well as stringent measures against judicial corruption, is crucial for restoring public trust.

4. **Public Perception**: The effectiveness of the judiciary in combating corruption also depends on public perception. If citizens believe that the judiciary is complicit in corrupt practices or is unable to deliver justice, it can erode trust in the entire democratic system.

The judiciary plays a vital role in controlling and facilitating corruption in India. By upholding the Constitution, enforcing anti-corruption laws, and protecting whistleblowers, the judiciary can act as a bulwark against corruption. However, to fulfill its mandate effectively, it must maintain its independence, address systemic challenges, and restore public faith in its integrity. Strengthening the judiciary is essential for ensuring that it remains an effective instrument for combating corruption and promoting accountability in governance.

Impact of Corruption on Citizens

Corruption is often described as a cancer that undermines the health of societies and economies. It manifests in various forms, from petty bribery to grand corruption involving politicians and powerful business interests, and it can have devastating effects on the lives of ordinary citizens. This section explores the multifaceted impact of corruption on citizens, examining its consequences on governance, social equity, economic development, and public trust.

1. Erosion of Trust in Governance

One of the most significant impacts of corruption is the erosion of trust in government institutions. When citizens perceive that their leaders are corrupt, they become disillusioned with the political system. This disillusionment can lead to apathy, voter disengagement, and lower participation in democratic processes. Citizens may feel that their voices do not matter, leading to a cycle of disengagement and further entrenchment of corrupt practices.

Moreover, when public officials engage in corrupt activities, it sends a message that the rule of law is not equally applied, creating a perception of injustice. This can undermine the legitimacy of government institutions and hinder efforts to promote good governance and accountability.

2. Degradation of Public Services

Corruption has a direct impact on the quality and accessibility of public services. When public funds meant for education, healthcare, infrastructure, and social welfare are siphoned off through corrupt practices, citizens are left to bear the brunt of inadequate services.

1. **Healthcare**: In the healthcare sector, corruption can manifest as bribery for access to medical services, manipulation of procurement processes, and misallocation of resources. Patients may be forced to pay bribes to receive timely medical care, leading to worse health outcomes, especially for the economically disadvantaged.

2. **Education**: In the education sector, corruption can result in the misappropriation of funds intended for schools, leading to dilapidated infrastructure, lack of teaching materials, and underpaid teachers. This degradation affects the quality of edu-

cation received by students, limiting their future opportunities and perpetuating cycles of poverty.

3. **Infrastructure**: Corruption can hinder infrastructure development as funds allocated for public works are diverted for personal gain. This can lead to poorly constructed roads, inadequate public transportation, and unsafe buildings, directly impacting citizens' quality of life.

3. Economic Consequences

Corruption stifles economic growth and perpetuates inequality. It creates an environment where businesses must navigate a maze of bureaucratic hurdles, often resorting to bribery to secure contracts or permits. This not only increases the cost of doing business but also deters foreign investment and stifles entrepreneurship.

1. **Inefficiency and Waste**: Corruption leads to misallocation of resources, as projects may be approved based on personal gain rather than public need. This inefficiency translates into suboptimal economic performance, as funds are wasted on non-productive ventures.

2. **Increased Costs of Goods and Services**: As businesses pass on the costs of bribery and corruption to consumers, the prices of goods and services rise. This disproportionately affects low-income citizens who spend a larger portion of their income on basic necessities, further entrenching poverty and inequality.

3. **Job Creation and Economic Mobility**: Corruption limits job creation by creating an uneven playing field where businesses that engage in corrupt practices thrive at the expense of those that operate ethically. This diminishes economic mobility for citizens who lack the means to engage in or navigate corrupt systems.

4. Social Inequity and Marginalization

Corruption exacerbates existing social inequalities and marginalizes vulnerable communities. Those who are already disadvantaged—such as women, lower castes, and economically weaker sections—are often the most affected by corrupt practices. They may lack the resources to pay bribes, leading to further exclusion from essential services and opportunities.

1. **Marginalization of Vulnerable Groups**: Corruption can limit access to resources and opportunities for marginalized groups, perpetuating cycles of poverty and disenfranchisement. This can lead to social unrest and tensions between different community groups.
2. **Impact on Women**: Women often face unique challenges in corrupt systems, as they may be subject to additional barriers when seeking access to services or economic opportunities. Gender-based discrimination compounded by corruption can further restrict women's participation in public life and economic development.

5. Psychological Impact

The pervasive nature of corruption can lead to a sense of helplessness among citizens. When people feel that they cannot rely on public institutions to serve their needs fairly, it can lead to a range of psychological effects, including frustration, anger, and resignation. This psychological burden can further discourage civic engagement and participation in governance.

The impact of corruption on citizens is profound and far-reaching. It undermines trust in institutions, degrades public services, hampers economic development, exacerbates social inequalities, and inflicts psychological harm. Addressing corruption requires a concerted effort from all stakeholders, including government, civil society, and citizens themselves. Promoting transparency, accountability, and active citizen engagement are essential steps toward rebuilding trust and creating a more equitable and just society for all.

Conclusion: The Need for Vigilance

Political corruption is a systemic issue that affects all aspects of governance, public services, and the daily lives of Indian citizens. While efforts have been made to combat corruption—through stronger laws, public interest litigations, and media vigilance—corruption continues to undermine the effectiveness of governance.

For young citizens, understanding the role of corruption in politics is crucial. It not only helps them identify how political decisions shape their lives but also empowers them to demand greater transparency, accountability, and fairness from their leaders. The fight against corruption is not a partisan issue—it affects everyone, regardless of party or ideology. Therefore, it is vital for all Indians, especially the youth, to be vigilant and proactive in seeking a more transparent and corruption-free political system.

| 7 |

Anti-Corruption Movements and Reforms

Corruption has long been a part of India's political landscape, but it has also faced strong resistance from civil society, activists, and reformist politicians. Over the years, several notable anti-corruption movements and reforms have emerged to tackle the problem head-on. These movements and initiatives have not only exposed corrupt practices but also empowered citizens to demand more transparency and accountability from their leaders. In this chapter, we explore key anti-corruption movements, the government's responses, and reforms that have aimed to cleanse the system.

Anti-Corruption Movements in India

Corruption has been a persistent challenge in India, affecting every stratum of society and governance. Over the years, various movements have emerged to combat this malaise, highlighting the citizens' desire for transparency, accountability, and justice. This section delves into the key anti-corruption movements in India, tracing their origins, objectives, and impacts, with a focus on notable figures and milestones.

1. Historical Context

India's struggle against corruption can be traced back to the colonial era, where rampant corruption in British administration sparked discontent among the populace. Post-independence, the expectation was that the new democratic government would be free from the corruption that characterized colonial rule. However, as years went by, systemic corruption began to infiltrate various levels of governance, leading to a series of movements aimed at rooting out corrupt practices.

2. The Role of Civil Society

Civil society organizations and activist groups have played a crucial role in raising awareness about corruption and mobilizing public sentiment against it. These groups have often acted as watchdogs, exposing corrupt practices and demanding accountability from public officials. Movements like the India Against Corruption (IAC) gained prominence through grassroots activism and extensive media coverage, galvanizing citizens across the nation.

3. The Jan Lokpal Movement

One of the most significant anti-corruption movements in recent Indian history is the Jan Lokpal Movement, which gained momentum in 2011. Spearheaded by social activist Anna Hazare, the movement sought the establishment of an independent and powerful Lokpal (Ombudsman) to investigate and prosecute corruption at all levels of government.

Key Features of the Jan Lokpal Movement:

- **Public Hunger Strike**: Anna Hazare's hunger strike at Jantar Mantar in Delhi in April 2011 drew massive crowds and media attention, creating a nationwide dialogue about corruption. The strike highlighted the demand for a Lokpal Bill that would empower an independent body to address corruption complaints against public officials.
- **Mass Mobilization**: The movement saw unprecedented public participation, with citizens from various walks of life rallying

in support of the cause. This widespread engagement demonstrated a collective desire for transparency and accountability.

- **Political Impact:** The Jan Lokpal Movement influenced political discourse, prompting the government to introduce the Lokpal Bill in Parliament. Although the initial version of the Bill faced criticism for being diluted, the movement highlighted the urgent need for systemic reforms.

4. The Right to Information (RTI) Act

The Right to Information Act, enacted in 2005, is a significant legislative achievement in India's fight against corruption. The RTI Act empowers citizens to seek information from public authorities, promoting transparency and accountability. Activists and citizens have utilized this law to expose corruption and maladministration, making it an essential tool in the anti-corruption arsenal.

Key Aspects of the RTI Movement:

- **Grassroots Empowerment:** The RTI movement encouraged ordinary citizens to actively participate in governance by seeking information about public expenditures and government functioning. This empowerment has led to increased vigilance and scrutiny of government actions.
- **Impact on Corruption:** Numerous cases of corruption have been exposed through RTI applications, leading to investigations and legal action against corrupt officials. The law has played a pivotal role in creating a culture of accountability.

5. Recent Movements and Trends

In recent years, anti-corruption movements have continued to evolve, addressing contemporary issues and leveraging technology to enhance their reach and effectiveness.

1. **Youth-led Movements:** Young activists have increasingly taken up the mantle of anti-corruption advocacy, utilizing so-

cial media to mobilize support and raise awareness. Campaigns against corruption have gained traction among the youth, highlighting their role in shaping the future of governance.

2. **Digital Activism**: The rise of digital platforms has enabled activists to spread their message quickly and engage a broader audience. Online petitions, social media campaigns, and digital advocacy have become powerful tools for anti-corruption movements.

3. **Environmental and Social Justice Movements**: Many anti-corruption campaigns have intersected with movements advocating for environmental protection and social justice. Activists have highlighted how corruption in governance often leads to environmental degradation and socio-economic disparities, thus framing corruption as a multifaceted issue.

6. Challenges Faced by Anti-Corruption Movements

Despite the progress made by anti-corruption movements, several challenges persist:

- **Political Resistance**: Many political leaders may resist reforms that threaten their power or expose corrupt practices, leading to pushback against anti-corruption initiatives.
- **Limited Implementation of Reforms**: While laws like the RTI Act and the Lokpal Bill have been established, the effective implementation of these reforms remains a challenge, often hampered by bureaucratic inertia and lack of political will.
- **Public Apathy**: Although there is widespread discontent regarding corruption, public engagement in anti-corruption movements can be inconsistent. Apathy or resignation among citizens can hinder sustained pressure for change.

Anti-corruption movements in India have emerged as vital expressions of public dissent against corruption and maladministration. They have galvanized citizens, influenced political discourse, and contributed to significant legislative changes. However, the struggle against corruption is ongoing, requiring continuous vigilance, public engagement, and a commitment to reform from all sectors of society. As citizens become increasingly aware of their rights and the power of collective action, the fight against corruption can pave the way for a more transparent and accountable governance framework in India.

Other Grassroots Anti-Corruption Movements

While the Jan Lokpal Movement and the Right to Information (RTI) Act are among the most recognized anti-corruption initiatives in India, numerous other grassroots movements have emerged across the country, driven by local communities, civil society organizations, and passionate individuals. These movements have played a crucial role in addressing corruption at various levels of governance and advocating for accountability and transparency. Here, we explore some notable grassroots anti-corruption movements that have made a significant impact in their regions.

1. Bihar's Anti-Corruption Movement

In Bihar, grassroots activists and local organizations have taken a stand against corruption, particularly in the context of welfare schemes. One notable initiative was led by the organization **Bihar Vikas Manch**, which aimed to expose the misuse of funds allocated for poverty alleviation programs.

Key Features:

- **Public Audits**: Activists conducted social audits to track the implementation of government schemes like the Mahatma Gandhi National Rural Employment Guarantee Act (MGNREGA). They uncovered discrepancies in fund allocation and identified corrupt officials, bringing these issues to the attention of the media and the public.
- **Mobilization of Local Communities**: The movement mobilized local communities to participate actively in the auditing

process, empowering them to demand accountability from local authorities.

2. Sikkim's Campaign Against Corruption

In Sikkim, a unique grassroots movement has emerged that focuses on combating corruption within the local government and ensuring the proper implementation of welfare schemes.

Key Features:

- **Engagement of Youth and Students**: The movement has seen significant involvement from students and young activists who organized campaigns and awareness programs to educate the public about their rights and the importance of transparency in governance.
- **Social Media Activism**: Utilizing platforms like Facebook and Twitter, activists have created online campaigns to raise awareness about corruption in local governance, drawing attention to specific cases of mismanagement and corruption.

3. Karnataka's Anti-Corruption Campaigns

In Karnataka, various grassroots organizations have emerged to tackle corruption, particularly in the context of public services and governance. The **Karnataka Jana Sahayog** movement is a notable example.

Key Features:

- **Whistleblower Protection**: This movement has actively promoted the need for legal protection for whistleblowers who expose corruption within government departments. This initiative has encouraged more individuals to come forward with information about corrupt practices.
- **Community Awareness Programs**: The movement conducts workshops and seminars to educate citizens about their rights,

the legal framework surrounding corruption, and the steps they can take to combat it.

4. Telangana's Fight Against Corruption

Telangana has witnessed a surge in grassroots anti-corruption activism, particularly following the formation of the state in 2014. Activists and organizations like the **Telangana Civil Society** have come together to address issues of corruption and governance.

Key Features:

- **Public Interest Litigations (PILs)**: Activists have filed PILs in the High Court to challenge corrupt practices and demand accountability from elected representatives and bureaucrats. These legal challenges have often led to investigations and reforms.
- **Community Participation**: The movement emphasizes the importance of community involvement in governance, encouraging citizens to participate in public meetings and demand transparency in government dealings.

5. Delhi's Anti-Corruption Initiatives

In the national capital, Delhi, several grassroots movements have emerged in response to corruption within local governance and public services.

Key Features:

- **Awareness Campaigns**: Organizations like **Kabir**, a civil society group, have conducted awareness campaigns to inform citizens about their rights under the RTI Act and how to effectively use it to expose corruption.
- **Protests and Demonstrations**: Regular protests and demonstrations have been organized to draw attention to specific cases of corruption, particularly related to public services like water supply and waste management.

6. The Role of Technology in Grassroots Movements

The advent of technology has transformed grassroots anti-corruption movements in India. Many activists have leveraged technology to enhance their efforts in various ways:

- **Digital Platforms**: Activists use social media and websites to organize campaigns, share information, and mobilize public support. Crowdsourcing platforms allow citizens to report corruption anonymously, leading to greater participation.
- **Data Analysis**: Some organizations utilize data analytics to track government spending and identify irregularities in the allocation of funds. This data-driven approach enhances the credibility of anti-corruption efforts and supports advocacy for reforms.

7. Challenges Faced by Grassroots Movements

While grassroots anti-corruption movements have made significant strides, they also face numerous challenges:

- **Political Backlash**: Activists often face threats and intimidation from corrupt officials and political leaders who perceive their efforts as a threat to their power. This can discourage individuals from participating in or supporting anti-corruption initiatives.
- **Resource Constraints**: Many grassroots movements operate on limited resources, making it challenging to sustain their activities or expand their reach. Financial constraints can hinder efforts to organize campaigns, conduct research, or engage in advocacy.
- **Public Apathy**: Despite widespread awareness of corruption, public apathy can pose a significant hurdle. Many citizens may feel disillusioned or powerless to effect change, leading to lower levels of participation in anti-corruption movements.

Grassroots anti-corruption movements in India represent a vital force in the ongoing struggle against corruption. Through community engagement, awareness-raising, and advocacy for transparency, these movements have empowered citizens to demand accountability and justice from their leaders. While challenges persist, the resilience and determination of grassroots activists continue to inspire hope for a corruption-free India. As more individuals join the fight, the collective power of grassroots movements can create a significant impact, fostering a culture of integrity and ethical governance across the nation.

Government Initiatives: Reforms to Combat Corruption

In response to the pervasive issue of corruption that has plagued India's political and administrative systems, the government has implemented several initiatives and reforms aimed at enhancing transparency, accountability, and efficiency in governance. These initiatives range from legislative measures to policy reforms and technological advancements, each designed to address specific aspects of corruption and promote ethical conduct in public life. This section explores key government initiatives that have been introduced to combat corruption effectively.

1. Right to Information (RTI) Act, 2005

One of the most significant legislative measures in the fight against corruption is the **Right to Information (RTI) Act**, enacted in 2005. This landmark legislation empowers citizens to seek information from public authorities, thereby promoting transparency and accountability in governance.

- **Empowering Citizens**: The RTI Act allows individuals to request information related to government functioning, decision-making processes, and financial dealings. By providing citizens with access to information, the act enables them to hold public officials accountable for their actions.

- **Impact on Corruption**: The RTI has proven instrumental in exposing corruption in various government departments. Numerous cases of misappropriation of funds and irregularities in project implementation have come to light through RTI queries, leading to administrative action against corrupt officials.
- **Challenges**: Despite its success, the implementation of the RTI Act faces challenges, including bureaucratic resistance, a lack of awareness among citizens, and attempts to undermine its provisions through amendments and litigation.

2. Lokpal and Lokayuktas Act, 2013

The establishment of an independent ombudsman, known as the **Lokpal**, was a crucial reform aimed at addressing corruption at high levels of government. The **Lokpal and Lokayuktas Act** was enacted in 2013 to create a statutory body that investigates allegations of corruption against public servants.

- **Functions of the Lokpal**: The Lokpal has the authority to receive complaints, conduct inquiries, and investigate cases of corruption against public officials, including the Prime Minister, ministers, and members of Parliament. It can also recommend prosecution in cases of proven misconduct.
- **State-Level Lokayuktas**: In addition to the Lokpal at the national level, the act encourages states to establish Lokayuktas to address corruption at the state level. This decentralized approach aims to enhance accountability within state governments.
- **Implementation Challenges**: Despite the Lokpal's establishment, the body has faced significant delays in its operationalization due to bureaucratic hurdles and political resistance. The effectiveness of the Lokpal continues to be a subject of debate, and there are calls for further strengthening its powers and independence.

3. Demonetization (2016)

In November 2016, the Indian government announced a sudden demonetization of ₹500 and ₹1,000 currency notes to combat black money and corruption. The move aimed to eliminate counterfeit currency and promote a digital economy.

- **Immediate Impact**: The demonetization policy aimed to disrupt the operations of corrupt individuals and entities holding unaccounted wealth. It sought to encourage the transition to cashless transactions, thus increasing transparency in financial dealings.
- **Long-Term Implications**: While the immediate impact on corruption was debated, the move pushed citizens and businesses to adopt digital payment methods, reducing the reliance on cash and enhancing traceability in financial transactions.
- **Criticism and Controversies**: Demonetization faced criticism for its abrupt implementation, leading to economic disruptions and hardship for the poor and middle class. Critics argued that it disproportionately affected small businesses and failed to achieve its primary goal of eradicating black money.

4. Goods and Services Tax (GST) Implementation (2017)

The introduction of the **Goods and Services Tax (GST)** in 2017 was another significant reform aimed at simplifying the tax structure and reducing corruption in the indirect taxation system.

- **Unified Tax System**: GST replaced multiple indirect taxes with a single tax, making the tax system more transparent and easier to administer. This reform aimed to reduce tax evasion and promote compliance among businesses.
- **Digital Compliance**: GST requires businesses to maintain digital records of transactions, facilitating real-time tracking of tax payments and reducing opportunities for corruption. The automated system minimizes human intervention in tax collec-

tion, thereby decreasing the chances of bribery and malpractices.

- **Challenges in Implementation**: While GST has improved transparency in tax administration, its implementation faced challenges such as technical glitches, compliance issues among small businesses, and the need for continuous training and awareness programs.

5. Digital India Initiative

The **Digital India** initiative launched in 2015 aims to transform India into a digitally empowered society and knowledge economy. This initiative plays a crucial role in combating corruption by promoting transparency and accountability in governance.

- **E-Governance and Service Delivery**: Through the Digital India initiative, various government services have been digitized, allowing citizens to access services online without intermediaries. This reduces opportunities for corruption by minimizing human interaction in service delivery.
- **Open Data Initiatives**: The government has promoted open data policies, encouraging the sharing of government data with the public. This transparency allows citizens and civil society organizations to monitor government spending and hold authorities accountable.
- **Cybersecurity and Privacy Concerns**: While digital initiatives have improved governance, they also raise concerns regarding data privacy and cybersecurity. Addressing these issues is vital to ensuring the integrity and security of digital governance.

6. Strengthening Anti-Corruption Agencies

The Indian government has taken steps to strengthen anti-corruption agencies such as the **Central Bureau of Investigation (CBI)** and the **Enforcement Directorate (ED)**. These agencies play a crucial role in investigating and prosecuting corruption cases.

- **Empowering Agencies**: Enhanced powers and resources have been allocated to these agencies to improve their effectiveness in tackling corruption. This includes better training, technology, and financial resources to conduct thorough investigations.
- **Public Confidence**: Strengthening anti-corruption agencies is essential to rebuilding public confidence in the government's commitment to tackling corruption. Effective prosecution of high-profile cases can serve as a deterrent to corrupt practices.

Government initiatives and reforms to combat corruption in India reflect a multi-faceted approach aimed at addressing the issue from various angles. From empowering citizens through the RTI Act to establishing robust mechanisms like the Lokpal and implementing digital governance, these initiatives seek to create a more transparent and accountable political system. However, challenges remain, and continuous efforts are needed to ensure the effective implementation of these reforms. As public awareness and participation grow, the collective demand for integrity and accountability can drive further change, leading to a corruption-free India.

The Road Ahead: Is Reform Enough?

The fight against corruption in India has been a long and arduous journey, marked by a myriad of challenges, movements, and reformative measures. While the initiatives discussed earlier represent significant steps toward addressing corruption, the question remains: **Is reform enough to eradicate this deep-rooted issue, or are more profound changes necessary?** This section explores the limitations of current reforms, the necessity for holistic approaches, and the potential paths forward in the ongoing battle against corruption.

1. Limitations of Existing Reforms

Despite the various reforms implemented in recent years, several limitations hinder their effectiveness in combating corruption:

- **Implementation Gaps**: Many laws and initiatives exist on paper but lack effective implementation. Bureaucratic inertia, lack of political will, and inadequate resources often prevent the successful execution of anti-corruption measures. For instance, while the RTI Act has empowered citizens, the resistance from certain government officials and the fear of repercussions can limit its impact.
- **Political Will and Accountability**: Corruption often thrives in an environment where political will is lacking. If politicians and parties are not genuinely committed to fighting corruption, reforms can become mere slogans without meaningful action. The politicization of anti-corruption agencies further complicates accountability, as these bodies may be used selectively against political adversaries rather than as impartial watchdogs.
- **Cultural Attitudes**: Corruption is often entrenched in societal norms and attitudes. A culture that accepts bribery as a means to navigate bureaucratic processes or views corruption as a necessary evil can undermine the effectiveness of reforms. Changing these cultural attitudes requires comprehensive public awareness campaigns and education initiatives aimed at fostering a culture of integrity and accountability.

2. Holistic Approaches to Combat Corruption

To effectively tackle corruption, a more holistic approach is necessary, incorporating multiple strategies that address both symptoms and root causes:

- **Strengthening Institutions**: Reforms should focus on strengthening institutions that promote good governance and transparency. This includes enhancing the autonomy and capacity of regulatory bodies, ensuring that they operate free from political interference, and providing them with the necessary resources to investigate and prosecute corruption cases effectively.

- **Promoting Civic Engagement**: Encouraging citizen participation in governance and decision-making processes can help create a more accountable political system. Civil society organizations, grassroots movements, and citizen forums can play a crucial role in monitoring government actions, advocating for transparency, and holding public officials accountable. Engaging the youth and empowering them to participate in political processes can lead to a more informed and active citizenry.

- **Judicial Reforms**: The judicial system must be reformed to ensure timely and fair justice in corruption cases. Delays in legal proceedings can lead to a lack of accountability and public trust in the system. Expediting trials, enhancing the capacity of judicial officers, and establishing special courts for corruption cases can improve the effectiveness of legal recourse.

- **Technology and E-Governance**: Embracing technology can play a pivotal role in enhancing transparency and reducing corruption. Digital platforms can streamline processes, reduce human interaction in service delivery, and provide citizens with easy access to information. Initiatives like blockchain technology can help create tamper-proof records, thereby minimizing opportunities for corruption.

3. The Role of Education and Awareness

Education is a critical component in the fight against corruption. Raising awareness about the detrimental effects of corruption on society, economy, and governance can foster a culture of integrity among citizens. Educational programs that emphasize ethical behavior, civic responsibility, and the importance of transparency can empower individuals to reject corrupt practices and demand accountability from their leaders.

4. International Collaboration

Corruption is often a transnational issue, requiring collaborative efforts between nations to combat effectively. International treaties, agreements, and cooperation among law enforcement agencies can help track and prosecute corrupt individuals and entities that operate across borders. Sharing best practices, technological solutions, and strategies can bolster global efforts against corruption.

5. Long-Term Vision and Commitment

Ultimately, the fight against corruption requires a long-term vision and commitment from all stakeholders, including government officials, civil society, the business community, and citizens. Anti-corruption efforts must be viewed not as isolated initiatives but as an integral part of a broader commitment to good governance, rule of law, and sustainable development.

In conclusion, while reforms are essential in addressing corruption, they are not sufficient on their own. A multifaceted approach that combines institutional strengthening, civic engagement, educational initiatives, and international collaboration is necessary to combat corruption effectively. The road ahead demands not only a commitment to reform but also a collective will to foster a culture of integrity and accountability in Indian society. Only through sustained efforts and a holistic strategy can India hope to build a corruption-free future, ensuring that its democracy thrives and its citizens can enjoy the fruits of good governance.

Conclusion: A Hopeful Future

As we conclude this chapter on anti-corruption movements and reforms in India, it is essential to reflect on the progress made and the road ahead. The fight against corruption is undeniably complex and challenging, but there are reasons for hope and optimism. While the journey has been fraught with setbacks, the persistent efforts of civil society, grassroots movements, and various government initiatives signal a growing recognition of the need for change.

1. Emerging Consciousness

One of the most promising aspects of the current landscape is the increasing awareness and consciousness among the Indian populace regarding the issue of corruption. Citizens are no longer passive observers; they are actively demanding accountability from their leaders and institutions. This shift is evident in the rise of social movements and protests that advocate for transparency and integrity. The willingness of ordinary citizens to stand up against corruption, as seen in movements like those led by Anna Hazare and others, signifies a collective resolve to reclaim democratic values.

2. Youth Empowerment

The youth of India play a crucial role in shaping the future, and their engagement in anti-corruption efforts is vital. With a significant portion of the population comprising young people, there is an immense potential for change. The new generation is more informed, tech-savvy, and connected than ever before, enabling them to leverage digital platforms to raise awareness, organize movements, and challenge corrupt practices. This spirit of activism and engagement bodes well for the future, as young leaders emerge to advocate for ethical governance and a transparent political process.

3. Institutional Reforms and Innovations

Recent reforms aimed at combating corruption reflect a growing recognition among policymakers of the need for systemic changes. Initiatives like the Right to Information (RTI) Act and the establishment of anti-corruption ombudsmen illustrate efforts to create mechanisms for transparency and accountability. Furthermore, the integration of technology in governance, such as e-governance initiatives and digital transactions, is transforming how public services are delivered, reducing opportunities for corruption at various levels.

4. Civil Society's Role

Civil society organizations continue to play a pivotal role in the fight against corruption. They act as watchdogs, advocating for transparency and holding public officials accountable. Through awareness campaigns, community mobilization, and policy advocacy, these organizations contribute significantly to creating a culture of integrity and ethical governance. Their efforts to engage with citizens and raise awareness about their rights empower individuals to participate actively in the democratic process.

5. Global Collaboration

In an increasingly interconnected world, the fight against corruption transcends national borders. Collaborative efforts among nations, international organizations, and civil society are crucial for addressing corruption that spans across jurisdictions. Initiatives that promote knowledge sharing, capacity building, and coordinated actions to tackle transnational corruption can bolster efforts at home and abroad. As India strengthens its engagement in global anti-corruption frameworks, it can draw upon best practices and experiences from other countries.

6. The Power of Hope and Determination

Ultimately, the road to a corruption-free India requires collective hope and determination. While challenges remain, it is essential to remain focused on the goal of creating a just and equitable society. The struggles against corruption should not be viewed as insurmountable obstacles but as opportunities for reform and renewal. With each movement, each protest, and each effort toward accountability, the foundations for a more transparent and responsive political system are being laid.

7. Looking Ahead

As we look ahead, it is crucial to continue pushing for reforms, supporting anti-corruption movements, and engaging in open dialogues about governance. The fight against corruption is ongoing, and while the path may be fraught with difficulties, each step taken toward transparency, accountability, and integrity brings us closer to the envisioned future. By fostering a collective commitment to these values, we can pave the way for a political culture that prioritizes the welfare of all citizens, ensuring that future generations inherit a democracy that thrives on integrity and trust.

In conclusion, while the battle against corruption may be long and arduous, there is ample reason to believe that a hopeful future is within reach. With sustained efforts, active participation, and an unwavering commitment to reform, India can emerge as a beacon of transparency and integrity, setting a precedent for others to follow. The journey towards this goal may be challenging, but together, as a united force, we can create the change we wish to see in our political landscape.

PART III: POWER GAMES AND POLARISATION

| 8 |

The Politics of Polarisation

Political polarisation refers to the growing ideological distance and antagonism between political parties, groups, and individuals. In recent years, this phenomenon has become increasingly pronounced in many democracies, including India, affecting the very fabric of societal cohesion and political discourse. Understanding the nature of political polarisation is essential to comprehend its implications for governance, social dynamics, and democratic integrity.

1. Defining Political Polarisation

At its core, political polarisation involves the division of society into sharply contrasting groups that often hold opposing views on key political issues. This divide can manifest in various forms, including ideological differences, policy preferences, and perceptions of social identity. In the Indian context, polarisation can be observed along multiple axes, including religion, caste, regional identities, and socio-economic status. These divides often lead to increased partisanship and hostility, diminishing the capacity for consensus and compromise.

2. Historical Context

Political polarisation is not a new phenomenon; its roots can be traced back to India's colonial past and the struggle for independence. The British employed a strategy of "divide and rule," exacerbating communal tensions between Hindus and Muslims, which laid the groundwork for future polarisation. Post-independence, the political landscape has continued to evolve, with various parties and movements leveraging existing divisions to consolidate power.

In the decades following independence, the rise of identity-based politics has played a significant role in deepening polarisation. Political parties have increasingly sought to mobilize support by appealing to specific identity groups, often at the expense of broader national unity. This approach has fostered an environment where the "us versus them" mentality thrives, further entrenching divisions within society.

3. Drivers of Polarisation

Several factors contribute to the increasing polarisation observed in contemporary Indian politics:

- **Identity Politics:** Political parties often exploit religious, caste, and regional identities to mobilize support. This strategy can reinforce existing divisions and create an environment of mistrust and animosity between groups.
- **Social Media and Technology:** The rise of digital platforms has transformed the way political discourse occurs. Social media algorithms tend to reinforce existing beliefs by creating echo chambers, where individuals are exposed primarily to viewpoints that align with their own. This phenomenon can exacerbate polarisation, as differing opinions are often dismissed or ridiculed.
- **Media Fragmentation:** The proliferation of media outlets catering to specific ideologies has contributed to the polarisation of public opinion. Partisan news sources often frame issues in ways that align with their ideological leanings, shaping public perceptions and reinforcing divisions.
- **Political Rhetoric:** Politicians frequently engage in inflammatory rhetoric that demonizes opponents and their supporters. This approach not only solidifies the loyalty of their base but also fosters hostility towards opposing viewpoints, further entrenching polarisation.

4. Consequences of Political Polarisation

The consequences of political polarisation are far-reaching and can undermine the democratic process:

- **Erosion of Civil Discourse:** Polarisation can stifle constructive dialogue and debate, as individuals become more entrenched in their views and less willing to engage with opposing perspectives. This breakdown in communication can hinder the ability to address complex societal issues effectively.
- **Increased Political Violence:** As divisions deepen, the risk of political violence and communal tensions rises. Historical instances of riots and violence in India often coincide with periods of heightened polarisation, where ideological differences escalate into physical confrontations.
- **Gridlock in Governance:** Polarisation can lead to legislative gridlock, as parties become unwilling to compromise or collaborate. This can hinder effective governance and policy-making, resulting in a lack of progress on pressing issues that require bipartisan support.
- **Threat to Democratic Values:** Ultimately, political polarisation poses a threat to the fundamental principles of democracy. When parties prioritize loyalty to their group over the common good, it can lead to a decline in public trust in institutions, eroding the foundations of democratic governance.

5. Addressing Political Polarisation

While the nature of political polarisation presents significant challenges, there are avenues for mitigating its effects:

- **Promoting Dialogue:** Encouraging open and respectful dialogue between opposing groups can help bridge divides. Initiatives aimed at fostering understanding and empathy can create spaces for constructive engagement.

- **Education and Awareness:** Educating citizens about the importance of diverse perspectives and the dangers of echo chambers can empower individuals to engage with differing viewpoints critically.
- **Strengthening Institutions:** A robust and impartial judiciary, along with transparent institutions, can play a crucial role in upholding democratic values and addressing grievances without succumbing to partisan pressures.
- **Civic Engagement:** Encouraging active civic participation can foster a sense of community and collective responsibility. Engaging citizens in decision-making processes can help rebuild trust in democratic institutions and counteract polarisation.

The nature of political polarisation in India reflects deep-seated historical, social, and ideological divides. While the challenges posed by polarisation are significant, understanding its roots and manifestations is crucial for navigating the complex political landscape. By promoting dialogue, education, and civic engagement, there is potential to bridge divides and foster a more inclusive and cohesive democratic society.

Divisive Politics: Caste, Religion, and Language as Tools of Polarisation

Divisive politics in India thrives on the manipulation of identity, particularly through caste, religion, and language. These elements are not merely social constructs; they are powerful tools that political actors exploit to mobilize support, create divisions, and establish dominance in a competitive electoral landscape. Understanding how caste, religion, and language function as tools of polarisation reveals the intricate dynamics of Indian politics and its impact on social cohesion.

1. Caste as a Tool of Polarisation

Caste has been a significant factor in Indian society for centuries, influencing social structure and relationships. The political landscape has not only acknowledged but also exploited caste differences to galvanize support.

- **Caste-Based Mobilization:** Political parties often use caste identities to consolidate votes. By aligning themselves with specific caste groups, parties can create strong, loyal voting blocs. This is particularly evident in states like Uttar Pradesh and Bihar, where caste dynamics heavily influence electoral outcomes. Leaders often appeal to caste sentiments, promising benefits or reservations that cater to specific groups, thereby deepening divisions.

- **Caste-Based Reservations:** The reservation system, initially intended to uplift marginalized communities, has been manipulated for electoral gain. Political leaders use promises of caste-based reservations as a means to secure votes, often leading to tensions between communities vying for limited resources and opportunities. The Mandal Commission's recommendations, which expanded reservations for Other Backward Classes (OBCs), exemplify how caste considerations can spark widespread political mobilization and social unrest.

- **Caste Alliances:** The formation of caste alliances is another strategy employed by political parties to enhance their electoral prospects. By grouping together various castes under a single political umbrella, parties aim to maximize their support base. This often results in a fragmented political landscape where caste loyalties overshadow broader national issues, reinforcing divisions within society.

2. Religion as a Tool of Polarisation

Religion plays a pivotal role in shaping political identities and allegiances in India. The complex interplay of religious sentiments and political ambition often leads to the exploitation of religious identities for electoral gains.

- **Communal Politics:** Politicians frequently resort to communal politics, invoking religious sentiments to polarize voters. The rhetoric surrounding religious identity can foster division, as political leaders seek to mobilize their base by emphasizing perceived threats from other communities. Events like the Babri Masjid demolition in 1992 and the subsequent riots exemplify how religious identities can be manipulated to incite violence and deepen divisions.

- **Appeasement and Alienation:** Political parties often engage in appeasement politics, where they cater to specific religious groups, particularly minority communities, to secure votes. This practice can alienate majority communities, leading to a perception of favoritism and exclusion. The resulting cycle of appeasement and alienation can exacerbate religious tensions, making it difficult to foster a sense of national unity.

- **Hindutva and Religious Nationalism:** The rise of Hindutva as a political ideology has significantly shaped the discourse around religion in politics. Parties like the Bharatiya Janata Party (BJP) have employed Hindutva to create a sense of Hindu identity that often marginalizes minority communities. This form of religious nationalism has intensified polarisation, as it frames political discourse in terms of religious identity rather than inclusive national identity.

3. Language as a Tool of Polarisation

Language is another powerful tool used in Indian politics to create divisions and mobilize support. India's linguistic diversity, while a source of cultural richness, has also been a point of contention.

- **Linguistic Identity Politics:** Political parties often appeal to linguistic identities to galvanize support at the regional level. This strategy is evident in states like Tamil Nadu and Maharashtra, where regional parties capitalize on linguistic pride and cultural identity to consolidate their voter base. For instance, the DMK and AIADMK in Tamil Nadu have historically leveraged the Tamil language and identity to mobilize support against perceived impositions from the central government.

- **Language as a Barrier:** Language can also serve as a barrier to national integration, with linguistic differences exacerbating regional disparities. In some cases, the imposition of Hindi as a national language has led to resistance and resentment in non-Hindi-speaking states, fueling regionalist sentiments. This linguistic divide can complicate governance and foster an "us versus them" mentality among different linguistic groups.
- **Regionalism and Language Politics:** Regional parties often exploit language as a rallying point for mobilizing support against national parties. The assertion of regional linguistic identity can lead to demands for autonomy or even secession, as seen in movements for statehood based on linguistic lines. Such assertions often result in heightened tensions between states and the central government, complicating the already intricate fabric of Indian politics.

4. Consequences of Divisive Politics

The use of caste, religion, and language as tools of polarisation has profound implications for Indian society and democracy:

- **Erosion of National Unity:** Divisive politics undermines the very foundation of a cohesive national identity. The emphasis on identity politics can fragment society into competing groups, weakening the sense of shared citizenship and collective purpose.
- **Increased Social Tensions:** The manipulation of caste, religion, and language can lead to increased social tensions and conflicts. Historical instances of communal violence and caste-related riots highlight the potential for divisive politics to escalate into violent confrontations.

- **Obstruction of Governance:** Polarisation complicates governance, as political parties become entrenched in their identities and are less willing to collaborate across party lines. This can result in legislative gridlock and hinder effective policymaking, ultimately affecting citizens' welfare.
- **Threat to Democratic Values:** When political parties prioritize identity politics over the common good, democratic values are undermined. The emphasis on divisive narratives can lead to a decline in public trust in institutions and a weakened commitment to democratic principles.

Divisive politics, driven by the manipulation of caste, religion, and language, poses significant challenges to the unity and stability of Indian democracy. While identity is an essential part of social life, its exploitation for political gain can lead to dangerous consequences. Addressing the challenges posed by divisive politics requires a concerted effort to promote inclusive narratives that transcend identity boundaries and foster a sense of belonging among all citizens. Through dialogue, education, and active engagement, there is potential to counter the forces of polarisation and work towards a more unified and resilient democratic society.

Consequences of Political Polarisation

Political polarisation refers to the growing ideological and emotional distance between political groups, leading to an increasingly divided society. In India, where the political landscape is shaped by diverse identities, including caste, religion, and language, the consequences of polarisation are profound and multifaceted. This phenomenon can significantly affect social cohesion, governance, and the overall health of democracy. Below are the major consequences of political polarisation in India:

1. Erosion of National Unity

One of the most significant consequences of political polarisation is the erosion of national unity. As parties and leaders increasingly align with specific identity groups, the sense of belonging to a larger national community diminishes. This fragmentation undermines the very fabric of Indian democracy, which is built on the principles of pluralism and inclusivity.

- **Diminished Sense of Belonging:** When political discourse focuses on divisive identities rather than common interests, individuals may feel alienated from the national narrative. This can lead to a loss of faith in democratic institutions and a decline in civic engagement, as people identify more strongly with their caste, religion, or linguistic group than with the nation.
- **Increased Regionalism:** Polarisation often gives rise to heightened regionalism, where states or communities prioritize their interests over national goals. This can result in conflicts over resources, policy decisions, and cultural recognition, further fragmenting the national identity.

2. Increased Social Tensions and Conflict

Political polarisation can exacerbate social tensions, leading to communal violence, caste-based conflicts, and social unrest. The amplification of identity politics often paves the way for hostility and distrust among different groups.

- **Communal Violence:** Historical instances of communal riots in India demonstrate how polarised political rhetoric can incite violence. Events like the Gujarat riots of 2002 and the Delhi riots of 2020 reveal the dangerous potential for polarisation to escalate into large-scale violence, disrupting social harmony and causing significant loss of life and property.
- **Caste Conflicts:** The competition for political power often plays out in the form of caste conflicts. Political parties that exploit caste identities may provoke tensions among different

groups, leading to clashes and unrest. The rise of caste-based movements seeking reservations or political recognition can further intensify these conflicts.

3. Obstruction of Governance and Policy-Making

Polarisation complicates the functioning of democratic institutions and hampers effective governance. When political parties become entrenched in their identities, collaboration across party lines becomes challenging, leading to legislative gridlock and stalled policy initiatives.

- **Legislative Gridlock:** Political polarisation can result in a lack of consensus on critical issues, making it difficult for governments to pass legislation. This gridlock can hinder the implementation of essential reforms and policies, impacting public welfare and development.
- **Reduced Accountability:** When political loyalty supersedes accountability, elected officials may prioritize the interests of their identity group over the broader public good. This can lead to corruption, nepotism, and a lack of transparency in governance, as parties focus on consolidating their power rather than serving the interests of all citizens.

4. Threat to Democratic Values and Institutions

The rise of polarisation poses a significant threat to the core values of democracy, including tolerance, dialogue, and pluralism. When political discourse becomes hostile and combative, the principles of democratic engagement are undermined.

- **Decline of Civil Discourse:** Polarisation fosters an environment where civil discourse is replaced by hostility and aggression. Political debates become increasingly charged, with individuals unwilling to engage with opposing viewpoints. This decline in respectful dialogue undermines the democratic

process and discourages meaningful debate on important issues.

- **Erosion of Trust in Institutions:** As polarisation intensifies, public trust in democratic institutions diminishes. Citizens may perceive institutions like the judiciary, election commissions, and law enforcement as biased or ineffective, leading to disillusionment with the political system. This erosion of trust can further alienate citizens from active participation in democracy.

5. Radicalization of Political Discourse

Political polarisation can lead to the radicalization of political discourse, where moderate voices are drowned out by extreme ideologies. This radicalization can manifest in several ways:

- **Normalization of Extremism:** Polarisation often legitimizes extreme views, pushing mainstream parties to adopt more radical positions to appease their bases. This shift can result in the marginalization of moderate voices and increase the appeal of extremist parties and movements.
- **Rise of Populism:** The divide between 'us' versus 'them' can give rise to populist leaders who exploit fears and grievances to gain support. Populism often simplifies complex issues into binary narratives, appealing to emotions rather than rational discourse. This can further entrench divisions and lead to unstable political environments.

6. Impact on Policy Formulation and Implementation

The consequences of political polarisation extend to policy formulation and implementation. When political parties prioritize identity over common good, policies may reflect divisive interests rather than holistic development.

- **Neglect of Public Interests:** Political leaders may focus on policies that cater to specific groups, neglecting broader public interests. This can lead to imbalanced development, where certain communities receive preferential treatment while others are marginalized.

- **Difficulty in Addressing Socio-Economic Issues:** Polarised politics can make it challenging to address critical socio-economic issues such as poverty, education, and healthcare. Policies aimed at fostering equitable development may be sidelined in favor of initiatives that cater to the interests of dominant identity groups, ultimately hindering national progress.

The consequences of political polarisation in India are far-reaching, affecting social cohesion, governance, and democratic values. As society becomes increasingly divided along identity lines, the challenges to national unity and democratic integrity intensify. Addressing these consequences requires a collective effort to promote inclusivity, dialogue, and understanding across different groups. By fostering a culture of cooperation and mutual respect, it is possible to counteract the forces of polarisation and work towards a more united and resilient democratic society.

The Role of the Media in Polarisation

The media plays a crucial role in shaping public perception, influencing political discourse, and framing the narratives that drive political engagement. In the context of political polarisation, the media can either bridge divides or exacerbate them. In India, the evolution of media—ranging from traditional outlets like newspapers and television to modern platforms such as social media—has significantly impacted the political landscape and contributed to polarisation in various ways.

1. Framing and Narrative Building

Media outlets have the power to frame political events and issues in ways that resonate with specific audiences. This framing can reinforce existing biases and create an "us vs. them" mentality among different identity groups.

- **Selective Coverage:** News outlets may selectively cover events or issues that align with their political leanings, thereby reinforcing the narratives of particular groups. For example, if a media organization predominantly reports on the grievances of a specific community while downplaying the concerns of others, it can intensify divisions and polarise public opinion.
- **Sensationalism:** Sensationalist reporting can exacerbate polarisation by focusing on extreme viewpoints or conflicts rather than presenting balanced perspectives. When media prioritizes sensational stories, it often distorts public understanding of complex issues, leading to heightened emotions and reactions among the audience.

2. Echo Chambers and Confirmation Bias

The rise of digital media has led to the emergence of echo chambers—environments where individuals are exposed predominantly to information that reinforces their existing beliefs.

- **Social Media Algorithms:** Platforms like Facebook and Twitter use algorithms that tailor content to users' preferences. This can create echo chambers where users are primarily exposed to viewpoints that align with their own. Such environments encourage confirmation bias, wherein individuals dismiss contrary opinions and engage only with information that validates their beliefs, further entrenching polarisation.
- **Fragmentation of News Sources:** The proliferation of news sources and alternative media has contributed to a fragmented information landscape. As audiences gravitate towards outlets that share their ideological leanings, it becomes increasingly difficult to foster a common understanding of political issues. This fragmentation can lead to divergent realities, where dif-

ferent groups perceive entirely different narratives about the same event.

3. Manipulation and Misinformation

The spread of misinformation and disinformation is a significant concern in the current media landscape, particularly during election periods or major political events.

- **Fake News and Propaganda:** The intentional dissemination of false information can manipulate public opinion and fuel polarisation. Political actors may exploit media platforms to spread propaganda, mislead the public, or discredit opponents. This manipulation can create confusion and distrust, further deepening divisions among groups.
- **Lack of Accountability:** The rise of citizen journalism and unregulated platforms has made it easier for misinformation to spread without proper fact-checking. In the absence of robust editorial standards, false narratives can proliferate, leading to public outrage and exacerbating polarised sentiments.

4. Role of Traditional Media

While digital media has transformed the information landscape, traditional media outlets continue to play a significant role in shaping political discourse.

- **Influence of Editors and Journalists:** The editorial choices made by journalists and news organizations can influence public perceptions of political issues. Editorial slants or biased reporting can lead to a skewed understanding of political events and contribute to polarisation. For instance, if mainstream media portrays a particular community in a negative light during times of conflict, it can foster resentment and division.
- **Public Trust in Media:** Trust in traditional media has been declining, leading to increased reliance on alternative sources

of information. When audiences perceive traditional media as biased or untrustworthy, they may seek out less credible sources that align with their beliefs, further entrenching polarisation.

5. Media as a Platform for Dialogue

Despite its role in polarisation, media can also serve as a platform for dialogue and understanding among diverse communities.

- **Promoting Diverse Perspectives:** When media outlets provide space for a range of viewpoints and foster constructive conversations, they can help bridge divides. Platforms that encourage open dialogue and highlight common interests can contribute to a more nuanced understanding of complex political issues.

- **Fact-Checking and Accountability:** Initiatives focused on fact-checking and accountability can mitigate the effects of misinformation and promote informed discourse. By holding political actors accountable and providing accurate information, the media can play a vital role in countering polarisation.

6. The Future of Media and Polarisation

As media continues to evolve, its role in political polarisation will remain dynamic. The challenge lies in promoting responsible journalism that prioritizes accuracy and inclusivity.

- **Encouraging Media Literacy:** Enhancing media literacy among the public is essential to combating polarisation. When individuals are equipped with the skills to critically evaluate information, they are less susceptible to manipulation and misinformation. Educational initiatives that promote media literacy can help foster a more informed citizenry capable of engaging in constructive political discourse.

- **Promoting Ethical Journalism:** Media organizations must prioritize ethical journalism and strive for balanced reporting.

By fostering a commitment to impartiality and accuracy, the media can contribute to a healthier political environment and mitigate the effects of polarisation.

The role of the media in political polarisation is multifaceted and significant. While media can exacerbate divisions through framing, echo chambers, and misinformation, it also has the potential to foster dialogue and promote understanding. As India navigates the complexities of its diverse political landscape, the media's influence on polarisation will remain a critical area of focus. By embracing responsible journalism and prioritizing inclusivity, the media can contribute to a more united and resilient democratic society.

Conclusion: Overcoming the Politics of Polarisation

As India stands at the crossroads of social change and political evolution, the urgency to address and overcome the politics of polarisation has never been more pronounced. The growing divides along caste, religion, and regional identities pose significant challenges to national unity and democratic governance. However, recognizing the implications of polarisation and actively working towards mitigating its effects can pave the way for a more cohesive and resilient society.

1. Fostering Dialogue and Understanding

One of the most effective strategies to combat polarisation is to foster open dialogue and mutual understanding among diverse groups. Initiatives that encourage conversations between communities can help bridge divides by addressing misconceptions and building empathy.

- **Community Engagement:** Organizing community forums and workshops that bring together individuals from different backgrounds can create spaces for dialogue. Such interactions allow people to share their stories, experiences, and perspectives, fostering a sense of shared humanity that transcends divisive identities.

- **Educational Programs:** Schools and educational institutions play a pivotal role in shaping young minds. Introducing curricula that emphasize tolerance, inclusivity, and the importance of diverse perspectives can equip future generations with the tools needed to combat polarisation. By instilling values of empathy and respect, education can help cultivate a culture of dialogue and understanding.

2. Promoting Media Literacy and Critical Thinking

In an era dominated by information overload, media literacy is essential for combating polarisation. Educating citizens to critically evaluate information sources empowers them to discern facts from misinformation, thereby reducing the influence of polarising narratives.

- **Educational Initiatives:** Implementing media literacy programs in schools and communities can equip individuals with the skills to critically assess news and information. Workshops on fact-checking, identifying biases, and understanding media framing can enable citizens to navigate the complex media landscape more effectively.
- **Support for Responsible Journalism:** Encouraging media outlets to adhere to ethical journalism standards is crucial in combating polarisation. By prioritizing accuracy, balance, and accountability, media organizations can contribute to a more informed public discourse. Collaborative efforts between journalists and civil society organizations can promote fact-checking initiatives that enhance public trust in the media.

3. Political Accountability and Reforms

Political leaders and parties must take responsibility for their roles in perpetuating polarisation. Committing to transparent governance, ethical political practices, and accountability can help rebuild trust in political institutions.

- **Electoral Reforms:** Implementing electoral reforms that promote transparency in party funding and reduce the influence of money in politics can contribute to a healthier democratic environment. Ensuring fair representation and reducing the reliance on divisive strategies can foster a more inclusive political landscape.

- **Encouraging Cross-Party Collaboration:** Political parties must prioritize collaboration over competition, particularly on issues that transcend party lines. Building coalitions based on common goals rather than divisive identities can promote unity and foster a sense of shared purpose among citizens.

4. Strengthening Civil Society and Grassroots Movements

Civil society organizations and grassroots movements play a crucial role in advocating for social justice, equity, and inclusivity. Supporting and empowering these movements can drive positive change and counter polarising narratives.

- **Mobilizing Communities:** Grassroots movements that emphasize solidarity and collective action can unite individuals across divides. By addressing shared concerns, such as poverty, education, and health care, these movements can transcend identity politics and foster a sense of community.

- **Encouraging Civic Participation:** Engaging citizens in the political process through activism, volunteering, and advocacy can empower individuals to challenge polarising narratives. Encouraging young people to participate in democratic processes can create a more vibrant and representative political landscape.

5. Vision for a Unified Future

Overcoming the politics of polarisation requires a collective commitment to fostering unity while respecting diversity. The journey towards a cohesive society involves embracing the complexities of India's social fabric while working together to address common challenges.

- **Celebrating Diversity:** Recognizing and celebrating India's rich diversity can reinforce a sense of national identity that transcends divisive politics. Cultural exchange programs, interfaith dialogues, and community events can promote mutual respect and appreciation for different traditions and backgrounds.
- **Shared Goals for Progress:** Focusing on shared goals—such as economic development, education, and social justice—can unite citizens across divides. By emphasizing common aspirations and working collaboratively towards collective progress, individuals can transcend polarisation and build a brighter future for all.

Final Thoughts

The politics of polarisation is a formidable challenge that requires a concerted effort from individuals, communities, political leaders, and institutions. By fostering dialogue, promoting media literacy, ensuring political accountability, supporting civil society, and celebrating diversity, India can move towards a future that embraces unity and resilience. As citizens and leaders alike take responsibility for shaping the political landscape, the journey towards overcoming polarisation can lead to a more inclusive, equitable, and harmonious society. In this endeavor, hope and determination will be key drivers, inspiring action for a better tomorrow.

| 9 |

Power Dynamics between States and the Centre

In India's complex federal system, the interplay of power between states and the central government profoundly influences governance, economic development, and political dynamics across the country. This chapter delves into the intricate relationships, regional disparities, and power struggles that shape India's federal structure, highlighting their impact on state-level growth and autonomy.

Federalism in India: A Balancing Act

Federalism is a foundational principle of the Indian political system, embodying a complex relationship between the central government and the individual states. It is designed to accommodate the diverse needs of India's vast population while maintaining a unified national framework. This balancing act between state and central authority is crucial for managing the multifaceted social, cultural, and economic realities of the country.

1. Understanding Federalism

Federalism can be defined as a system of governance in which power is divided between a central authority and various constituent units, in this case, the states. This division allows each level of government to operate independently within its respective jurisdiction, yet it also necessitates cooperation and coordination to ensure effective governance.

- **Constitutional Framework:** The Indian Constitution lays the groundwork for federalism, delineating the powers and responsibilities of the central and state governments. The Constitution contains three lists—Union List, State List, and Concurrent List—which categorize the subjects on which each level of government can legislate. The Union List includes subjects of national importance, such as defense and foreign affairs, while the State List covers areas like police and public health. The Concurrent List allows both levels to legislate on subjects like education and marriage, creating a shared jurisdiction that requires collaboration.
- **Supremacy of the Constitution:** The Constitution is the supreme law of the land, providing the framework within which both central and state governments operate. Any legislation passed by either government must conform to the Constitution, ensuring that the rights and responsibilities of each level are upheld.

2. The Role of the Centre and the States

In India's federal structure, both the central and state governments play vital roles in governance, yet their powers and responsibilities can often overlap, leading to tensions and power struggles.

- **Powers of the Central Government:** The central government, often referred to as the Union government, holds significant authority, especially in matters that impact national integrity and security. It has the power to legislate on subjects that are crucial for maintaining unity, such as defense, foreign affairs, and interstate trade. Additionally, it can intervene in state affairs under certain circumstances, such as imposition of President's Rule in case of political instability.

- **Powers of the State Governments:** States possess their own set of powers, which allows them to address local issues effectively. They have the autonomy to legislate on matters such as health, education, agriculture, and local governance. This decentralization is crucial for addressing the unique challenges and aspirations of diverse regional populations, enabling states to respond to their citizens' needs more directly.

3. Challenges to Federalism

Despite the framework designed to maintain a balance between the central and state governments, various challenges threaten the functioning of federalism in India.

- **Centralization of Power:** Over the years, there has been a trend towards the centralization of power, where the central government has increasingly intervened in state matters. This centralization can undermine the autonomy of states and lead to feelings of disenfranchisement among state governments, particularly in regions that have distinct cultural or political identities.
- **Political Manipulation:** Political parties often use federalism as a tool for electoral gain. Central parties may attempt to undermine state governments led by rival parties, leading to political instability. Such tactics can result in the misuse of constitutional provisions, such as the imposition of President's Rule, which may be applied not necessarily for reasons of governance but for political expediency.
- **Resource Allocation:** Disparities in resource allocation from the central government to states can create friction. States with greater economic resources may feel marginalized if they do not receive an equitable share of central funding, leading to tensions that can exacerbate regional disparities and foster resentment.

4. Collaborative Federalism: A Path Forward

To navigate the complexities of federalism in India, a collaborative approach is essential. Both levels of government must work together to foster a more harmonious relationship that serves the interests of all citizens.

- **Inter-Governmental Dialogue:** Regular dialogue between the central and state governments can facilitate understanding and cooperation. Establishing forums for discussion, such as the Inter-State Council, allows states to voice their concerns and provide feedback on national policies. This collaborative framework can help mitigate conflicts and promote consensus-building.
- **Decentralized Decision-Making:** Encouraging decentralized decision-making empowers local governments and communities, ensuring that governance reflects the diverse needs and aspirations of citizens. By involving local bodies in planning and implementation, the government can create policies that are more attuned to regional realities.
- **Strengthening Fiscal Federalism:** Ensuring fair and transparent resource allocation is vital for promoting equitable development across states. Implementing mechanisms that distribute resources based on need rather than political considerations can help address regional disparities and foster a sense of inclusivity.

The Way Ahead

Federalism in India is a delicate balancing act that requires constant negotiation and adjustment between the central and state governments. As the country evolves, the dynamics of federalism must also adapt to reflect changing social, economic, and political landscapes.

The commitment to a cooperative federal framework can help ensure that both levels of government work in tandem to promote the welfare of citizens. By embracing the principles of collaboration, transparency, and equity, India can strengthen its federal structure and create a more unified, yet diverse, society. This commitment to balanced governance not only preserves the integrity of the nation but also empowers states to thrive within the framework of Indian federalism, ultimately benefiting the entire country.

Regional Disparities: Economic and Political Evolution

India is a vast and diverse country, home to a wide array of cultures, languages, and socio-economic conditions. The economic and political evolution of its states has been marked by significant regional disparities, which have shaped the country's development trajectory. Understanding these disparities is crucial for addressing the challenges and opportunities that arise in the context of India's federal structure.

1. Historical Context of Regional Disparities

India's colonial past has left an indelible mark on its economic and political landscape. The British colonial administration prioritized certain regions for resource extraction and infrastructure development, leading to uneven economic growth. For instance, areas rich in natural resources, such as coal and minerals, experienced different levels of investment compared to less resource-endowed regions.

- **Post-Independence Development:** After independence in 1947, the Indian government sought to address these disparities through various planning initiatives. However, early efforts were often hampered by a lack of local governance structures and capacity, resulting in the persistence of regional inequalities.

- **Green Revolution and Economic Policy:** The introduction of the Green Revolution in the 1960s brought about significant agricultural advancements but primarily benefited states with better irrigation and infrastructure, such as Punjab and Haryana, further widening the economic gap between regions.

2. Economic Disparities Across States

Economic disparities between states can be attributed to several factors, including geography, resource availability, industrialization, and investment in human capital.

- **Agricultural vs. Industrial Economies:** States like Punjab and Haryana have historically relied on agriculture, resulting in a strong agrarian economy. In contrast, states like Maharashtra and Gujarat have pursued industrialization aggressively, becoming hubs for manufacturing and trade. This shift has led to greater economic growth in industrialized states, attracting investments and creating job opportunities.
- **Infrastructure Development:** States with robust infrastructure—such as transportation, power supply, and communication networks—tend to attract more investments and experience higher rates of economic growth. For example, Maharashtra's developed infrastructure has made it a magnet for both domestic and foreign investments, while states like Bihar and Odisha, with underdeveloped infrastructure, have struggled to compete economically.
- **Human Capital and Education:** States that prioritize education and skill development, such as Kerala and Tamil Nadu, have seen a positive impact on their labor markets, leading to higher income levels and improved living standards. Conversely, states with lower educational attainment often face challenges in employment and economic participation, perpetuating cycles of poverty and underdevelopment.

3. Political Evolution and Regional Disparities

The political evolution of states in India has also been shaped by regional disparities. The rise of regional political parties has often been a response to perceived neglect by the central government and the need for local representation.

- **Emergence of Regional Parties:** In states with significant disparities, regional parties have emerged as powerful political forces, advocating for the interests of specific communities or regions. For instance, parties like the Dravida Munnetra Kazhagam (DMK) in Tamil Nadu and the Shiv Sena in Maharashtra have leveraged regional identity and aspirations to mobilize support and challenge national parties.
- **Policy Making and Representation:** Regional parties often bring local issues to the national stage, emphasizing the need for equitable resource allocation and development policies tailored to their specific contexts. This has led to a more decentralized approach to governance, where states demand greater autonomy and recognition of their unique challenges.

4. Impact of Central Policies on Regional Disparities

Central government policies have significantly influenced regional disparities, sometimes exacerbating existing inequalities while striving to promote balanced development.

- **Resource Allocation:** The distribution of central funds and resources has often been politically motivated, leading to accusations of favoritism. States governed by the ruling party may receive more funding and support for development projects compared to opposition-ruled states, creating an uneven playing field.
- **Economic Reforms:** Economic liberalization in the 1990s opened up new opportunities for growth but also highlighted existing disparities. While some states rapidly industrialized, others remained stagnant, prompting demands for more inclusive policies that address regional inequalities.

5. Strategies for Addressing Regional Disparities

To bridge the gaps between states and promote balanced development, several strategies can be implemented.

- **Balanced Development Policies:** The central government must adopt policies that prioritize balanced development, ensuring that underdeveloped states receive adequate resources and support for infrastructure, education, and health.
- **Decentralization and Local Governance:** Strengthening local governance structures can empower states to address their unique challenges effectively. Providing states with more autonomy in decision-making can lead to targeted policies that reflect local needs.
- **Investment in Human Capital:** Fostering education and skill development programs can enable states to harness their human resources, creating a more skilled workforce capable of participating in the global economy.

A Path Forward

Understanding the economic and political evolution of regional disparities in India is crucial for fostering national unity and inclusive growth. As India navigates its complex landscape, addressing these disparities through collaborative efforts between the central and state governments will be vital for ensuring equitable development. By promoting policies that consider the unique contexts of each state, India can work towards a more cohesive and prosperous future for all its citizens.

Power Struggles and Resistance to Central Authority

In India's federal structure, the distribution of power between the central government and state governments has often been a source of tension and conflict. These power struggles are influenced by historical, political, and socio-economic factors that shape the relationship between the center and the states. This section explores the dynamics of power struggles, the nature of resistance to central authority, and how these conflicts manifest in contemporary India.

1. Historical Context of Power Struggles

The power dynamics in India can be traced back to the colonial period when British governance centralized authority and marginalized local governance. Upon gaining independence in 1947, India adopted a federal structure, but the central government retained significant powers, especially in matters deemed crucial for national integrity and security.

- **The Constitution's Framework:** The Indian Constitution establishes a division of powers between the central government and state governments through the Union List, State List, and Concurrent List. While the intent was to create a balanced federal system, it often leads to disputes over jurisdiction, especially when states feel their rights are encroached upon.
- **Post-Independence Developments:** Over the years, major events such as the linguistic reorganization of states, the imposition of President's Rule in various states, and the central government's responses to regional demands have contributed to an evolving landscape of power struggles.

2. Contemporary Power Struggles

Power struggles between the central and state governments can manifest in various forms, including political, administrative, and fiscal conflicts.

- **Political Conflicts:** Political parties often play a significant role in shaping power dynamics. The central government's relationship with state governments can become contentious, especially when opposition parties are in power at the state level. This opposition can lead to conflicts over policy implementation and governance.

- **Example:** The rise of regional parties, such as the Trinamool Congress in West Bengal and the Aam Aadmi Party in Delhi, has often led to friction with the central government, particularly over issues like resource allocation and administrative autonomy.

- **Administrative Conflicts:** Administrative conflicts arise when the central government seeks to impose its directives on state administrations. States may resist policies that they perceive as undermining their autonomy or not aligned with local needs.
  - **Example:** The implementation of centrally sponsored schemes may face resistance from states that feel these schemes do not adequately consider local contexts or requirements.

- **Fiscal Conflicts:** Disputes over financial allocations and tax revenues are another significant area of conflict. States often demand a larger share of resources from the central government, especially for development projects and welfare schemes.
  - **Example:** The Goods and Services Tax (GST) implementation raised concerns among states regarding revenue-sharing and compensation mechanisms, leading to tensions between the central and state governments.

3. Resistance Movements and Autonomy Demands

Resistance to central authority often manifests through social movements, protests, and demands for greater autonomy. Several states and regions have witnessed movements that reflect their aspirations for self-governance and recognition of local identities.

- **Regional Autonomy Movements:** Various regions in India have demanded greater autonomy or statehood to address their unique socio-economic challenges. For instance, the demand for a separate state of Gorkhaland in West Bengal and the ongoing movements in Bodoland and other northeastern states highlight the desire for self-determination.

- **Protests Against Central Policies:** Grassroots movements often emerge in response to central government policies perceived as unjust or detrimental to local interests. Protests against the farm laws in 2020 are a prime example, where farmers from Punjab and Haryana resisted what they viewed as policies favoring corporate interests over their livelihoods.

- **Cultural and Linguistic Identity Movements:** Movements that assert regional identity, such as those led by linguistic groups or ethnic communities, challenge the central narrative and seek recognition and autonomy. For example, the demand for recognition of the Tamil language and culture in Tamil Nadu has long been a rallying point for regional political parties.

4. The Role of Political Parties

Political parties play a crucial role in shaping power struggles and resistance movements. Regional parties often capitalize on local sentiments and grievances, positioning themselves as champions of state rights against central authority.

- **Regional Party Dynamics:** Parties like the Shiv Sena in Maharashtra and the DMK in Tamil Nadu have leveraged regional identity to consolidate power and challenge the central government's authority. These parties often advocate for greater resource allocation and autonomy, tapping into local sentiments to mobilize support.

- **Coalition Politics:** The increasing trend of coalition politics has also influenced power dynamics. In a multi-party system, alliances between regional parties can significantly impact the central government's ability to govern effectively, as these parties often demand concessions in exchange for their support.

5. The Impact of Power Struggles on Governance

The ongoing power struggles and resistance to central authority have significant implications for governance in India. These conflicts can lead to policy paralysis, hinder development efforts, and create a sense of disenfranchisement among citizens.

- **Policy Implementation Challenges:** Frequent conflicts between the center and states can result in delays and complications in the implementation of policies and programs. This can adversely affect the delivery of essential services and welfare initiatives.
- **Erosion of Trust:** Continued power struggles may erode public trust in the political system, as citizens perceive their local leaders as unable to assert their rights against a dominant central government. This disillusionment can lead to apathy and disengagement from the political process.
- **Calls for Federalism Reform:** The persistent tensions have spurred discussions about the need for federalism reform in India. Advocates argue for a more equitable distribution of powers and resources, emphasizing the importance of cooperative federalism to enhance governance and address regional disparities.

Navigating Power Dynamics

The power struggles and resistance to central authority in India reflect the complexities of a diverse and democratic society. Understanding these dynamics is crucial for fostering a balanced federal system that respects the aspirations of both the central and state governments. As India continues to evolve, it will be essential to navigate these power dynamics through dialogue, cooperation, and a commitment to inclusive governance that considers the unique needs and challenges of all regions. By addressing the underlying issues that fuel these struggles, India can work towards a more harmonious and equitable political landscape, ultimately benefiting its citizens and the nation as a whole.

Cooperative Federalism and Challenges

Cooperative federalism refers to a system where the central and state governments work together to address common issues and achieve shared goals. In India, cooperative federalism is essential for promoting unity among the diverse states and ensuring that the benefits of governance reach all citizens. However, this approach also faces significant challenges that can impede effective collaboration between the two levels of government. This section will explore the concept of cooperative federalism in the Indian context, its importance, and the challenges it encounters.

1. Understanding Cooperative Federalism

Cooperative federalism in India emphasizes collaboration and partnership between the central and state governments. The Constitution of India envisages a framework where both levels of government have distinct but overlapping responsibilities, particularly in areas outlined in the Concurrent List. This model is designed to foster a sense of unity while respecting the autonomy of states.

- **Shared Responsibilities:** The spirit of cooperative federalism is evident in the distribution of responsibilities. While the central government handles national defense, foreign affairs, and monetary policy, states are responsible for education, health, and agriculture. Many issues, like public health and environmental protection, require joint efforts, thus necessitating cooperation.

- **Intergovernmental Institutions:** Various institutions facilitate cooperative federalism in India. The Finance Commission, the Planning Commission (now NITI Aayog), and the Inter-State Council serve as platforms for dialogue and collaboration between the center and states. These institutions aim to address fiscal disparities, resource allocation, and policy implementation.

2. Importance of Cooperative Federalism

Cooperative federalism is crucial for several reasons:

- **Addressing Regional Diversity:** India is characterized by its vast regional diversity in terms of culture, language, and economic development. Cooperative federalism allows for tailored solutions that consider local needs while ensuring a cohesive national framework.
- **Resource Sharing:** By working together, the central and state governments can pool resources to tackle common challenges, such as disaster management, health crises, and infrastructure development. This resource-sharing approach can lead to more efficient and effective governance.
- **Promoting Accountability:** Cooperative federalism encourages accountability and transparency in governance. Joint initiatives require both levels of government to report on their activities, fostering a culture of accountability among officials and institutions.
- **Conflict Resolution:** Cooperation can help mitigate conflicts that arise from competing interests between the center and states. Collaborative mechanisms can lead to negotiated settlements that consider the perspectives of both parties.

3. Challenges to Cooperative Federalism

Despite its importance, cooperative federalism in India faces several challenges that hinder effective collaboration between the central and state governments.

- **Centralization of Power:** One of the most significant challenges is the tendency toward centralization of power. The central government often exercises its authority in ways that undermine state autonomy, leading to conflicts. Policies that are perceived as overreach can create resentment among state governments, particularly those led by opposition parties.

Example: The central government's unilateral decision-making on critical issues, such as GST implementation and resource allocation for welfare schemes, has sometimes been met with resistance from states that feel sidelined.

- **Political Rivalries:** Political rivalries between the central and state governments can hamper cooperative efforts. When different political parties govern at the center and in various states, collaboration can become strained, as political agendas may diverge.

Example: The political opposition can lead to a lack of cooperation in implementing central policies, as seen during the farmer protests against the farm laws, where states governed by opposition parties resisted central directives.

- **Resource Allocation Disparities:** Disparities in resource allocation can create tensions. States often feel that they do not receive a fair share of revenue or resources from the central government, leading to dissatisfaction and conflict.

Example: The allocation of funds from the Finance Commission can be contentious, with states arguing for a more equitable distribution based on population, need, and developmental priorities.

- **Lack of Trust:** A lack of trust between the center and states can hinder cooperative federalism. When states perceive the central government as not acting in their best interests, it can lead to reluctance in collaboration.

Example: States may be hesitant to share data or resources with the central government if they fear misuse or a lack of transparency.

4. Strategies for Strengthening Cooperative Federalism

To address the challenges facing cooperative federalism in India, several strategies can be implemented:

- **Enhancing Dialogue:** Establishing regular forums for dialogue between the central and state governments can facilitate better communication, understanding, and collaboration. This can help build trust and resolve conflicts more effectively.
- **Decentralization of Powers:** Emphasizing the decentralization of powers can strengthen cooperative federalism. The central government should respect the autonomy of states and allow them to tailor policies to their specific contexts.
- **Transparent Resource Allocation:** Implementing transparent mechanisms for resource allocation can help alleviate tensions. Clear criteria for funding and resource distribution based on need and performance can foster cooperation.
- **Political Will:** Political leaders at both levels must demonstrate a commitment to cooperative federalism. By prioritizing collaboration over partisanship, leaders can work towards common goals that benefit citizens across the country.

Cooperative federalism is a vital component of India's political landscape, enabling the central and state governments to work together in addressing the diverse challenges facing the nation. While there are significant challenges to achieving effective cooperation, fostering a spirit of collaboration, transparency, and trust can lead to a more robust federal structure. Strengthening cooperative federalism will ultimately enhance governance, promote regional development, and ensure that the benefits of democracy reach all citizens, regardless of their geographic or socio-economic background.

Conclusion: Navigating Power Dynamics Between States and the Centre

The power dynamics between states and the central government in India are a complex interplay of cooperation, contention, and constitutional mandates. This chapter has explored the multifaceted nature of federalism in India, highlighting the delicate balance that exists between maintaining state autonomy and ensuring national cohesion. As India continues to evolve, it becomes increasingly important to understand the implications of these dynamics on governance, regional development, and citizen engagement.

1. The Essence of Federalism in India

At its core, federalism in India is designed to accommodate the country's vast diversity while promoting unity. The Constitution provides a framework that outlines the distribution of powers and responsibilities, yet the actual practice of federalism often varies significantly from the theoretical model. The evolution of federalism in India reflects not just the legal provisions but also the political realities shaped by historical contexts, regional aspirations, and the changing nature of governance.

2. Regional Disparities and Political Evolution

The political evolution of states such as Maharashtra, Tamil Nadu, and West Bengal illustrates how historical, cultural, and economic factors contribute to regional disparities. These states have developed distinct political identities, influenced by local issues, movements, and leadership styles. Understanding these nuances is crucial for policymakers to address regional inequalities effectively and ensure that the benefits of development are distributed equitably across the country.

3. Power Struggles and Resistance

The examples of power struggles and resistance to central authority—illustrated through farmer protests, regional autonomy movements, and demands for greater fiscal autonomy—underscore the tensions inherent in the federal structure. These movements are not merely reactions to policies but are also expressions of deeper sociopolitical sentiments that seek recognition and respect for regional identities and aspirations. Addressing these concerns requires a nuanced understanding of the local context and a willingness to engage in meaningful dialogue.

4. The Path Forward: Cooperative Federalism

As India navigates its complex federal landscape, the future of cooperative federalism is crucial. The ability of the central and state governments to collaborate effectively can determine the success of various governance initiatives and development projects. Promoting cooperative federalism involves not only institutional reforms but also a cultural shift towards mutual respect and collaboration between different levels of government.

5. Call for Reforms and Engagement

The challenges of power dynamics between the states and the center necessitate reforms that enhance transparency, accountability, and responsiveness in governance. This includes revisiting the distribution of resources, ensuring fair representation in intergovernmental institutions, and fostering greater public participation in decision-making processes. Engaging citizens in the political discourse is essential for building a more resilient and responsive federal structure.

In conclusion, the power dynamics between states and the central government in India are vital to understanding the nation's governance and development trajectories. By embracing the principles of cooperative federalism and addressing the challenges that arise, India can work towards a more inclusive and equitable political landscape. As the nation continues to evolve, the collaboration between the center and states will play a pivotal role in shaping the future of Indian democracy, ensuring that every citizen's voice is heard and respected.

| 10 |

The Politics of Change

In India, major political decisions have often sparked significant transformations across the socio-economic landscape, impacting millions of lives and shaping the nation's trajectory. This chapter explores pivotal moments of change driven by political decisions, including economic liberalization, demonetization, and farm bills. It also examines the crucial role of civil society and grassroots movements in influencing and responding to these changes.

Economic Liberalization: Opening India to Global Markets

Economic liberalization in India, which began in the early 1990s, marked a significant turning point in the country's economic landscape, fundamentally altering its relationship with global markets. This chapter delves into the motivations behind liberalization, the key reforms implemented, and the resulting impacts on various sectors of the economy, as well as the broader political implications.

1. Background and Motivations for Liberalization

Before the 1990s, India's economy was characterized by a mixed economy model with heavy state control over industries, extensive regulations, and a focus on self-sufficiency. The system, known as the "License Raj," led to inefficiencies, corruption, and stagnation, hindering economic growth and foreign investment.

By the late 1980s, several factors prompted a re-evaluation of this model:

- **Economic Crisis:** The balance of payments crisis of 1991 was a wake-up call for the Indian government. The country faced dwindling foreign exchange reserves and rising inflation, necessitating urgent action to stabilize the economy.
- **Global Trends:** The collapse of the Soviet Union and the global shift towards market-oriented economies underscored the need for India to adapt to a changing world. Many developing countries were successfully integrating into the global economy, and India risked being left behind.

These factors culminated in the decision to liberalize the economy, marking a departure from the previous protectionist policies.

2. Key Reforms Under Economic Liberalization

The liberalization process began in earnest with the implementation of several key reforms, which were primarily orchestrated by then-Finance Minister Dr. Manmohan Singh:

- **Deregulation:** The government dismantled the License Raj, reducing the number of industries requiring government approval to operate. This led to a surge in entrepreneurship and the establishment of new businesses.
- **Trade Liberalization:** Import tariffs were significantly reduced, allowing foreign goods to enter the Indian market. The introduction of the Export-Import Policy facilitated trade and opened up markets for Indian products abroad.
- **Foreign Direct Investment (FDI):** The government eased restrictions on foreign investments, encouraging multinational corporations to invest in various sectors such as telecommunications, automobiles, and information technology. The introduction of policies favoring FDI helped India attract billions of dollars in investment.

- **Privatization:** The disinvestment of state-owned enterprises aimed to reduce the financial burden on the government and improve efficiency. This process also encouraged private sector participation in previously state-controlled industries.
- **Financial Sector Reforms:** Reforms in the banking and financial sectors aimed to enhance efficiency and accessibility. The establishment of private banks and financial institutions increased competition and improved services for consumers.

3. Impact on Various Sectors

The liberalization of the Indian economy had profound effects across various sectors:

- **Information Technology:** The IT sector emerged as a global powerhouse, with Indian companies becoming leaders in software development and IT services. Cities like Bangalore became hubs for technology, attracting investment and talent from around the world.
- **Manufacturing:** Liberalization spurred growth in manufacturing industries, leading to increased production capabilities and job creation. The automotive and consumer goods sectors experienced significant growth, with both domestic and foreign companies setting up manufacturing facilities in India.
- **Agriculture:** Although agriculture was initially left out of the liberalization process, subsequent reforms aimed at improving efficiency, promoting exports, and enhancing the livelihoods of farmers became crucial. Initiatives like the National Agriculture Market (eNAM) aimed to integrate markets and provide farmers with better pricing.
- **Retail and Consumer Goods:** The entry of global retail giants revolutionized the retail landscape in India, leading to increased competition and variety for consumers. Local businesses had to adapt to changing consumer preferences and the rising demand for quality products.

4. Political Implications and Challenges

While economic liberalization led to significant growth and development, it also had important political implications:

- **Social Inequality:** The benefits of liberalization were not evenly distributed, leading to widening economic disparities between different regions and communities. This raised concerns about social justice and equity.
- **Political Resistance:** Liberalization faced resistance from various political factions, particularly those advocating for the rights of marginalized groups. Farmers' protests and labor movements emerged as voices against perceived inequities and the adverse effects of globalization.
- **Changing Political Landscape:** The rise of new economic interests transformed the political landscape, with emerging business leaders gaining influence. Political parties began to adapt their agendas to address the interests of a more diverse electorate shaped by economic changes.

A Path Forward

Economic liberalization has undeniably opened India to global markets and transformed its economic landscape. While it has led to remarkable growth and opportunities, the challenges associated with inequality and social justice must be addressed to ensure that the benefits of liberalization are inclusive and sustainable.

As India continues to navigate the complexities of a globalized economy, the lessons learned from the liberalization process will be vital in shaping future economic policies, promoting equitable growth, and fostering a more resilient and inclusive society.

Demonetization: Disrupting India's Cash Economy

On November 8, 2016, India witnessed one of the most significant economic upheavals in its recent history when Prime Minister

Narendra Modi announced the demonetization of ◊500 and ◊1,000 banknotes. This bold move aimed to tackle several pressing issues within the Indian economy, including corruption, black money, counterfeit currency, and the informal cash-driven economy. While the decision was lauded by some as a necessary step towards a cleaner economy, it also sparked widespread debate and controversy regarding its effectiveness and implications. This section delves into the motivations behind demonetization, its execution, immediate impacts, and the ongoing discussions about its long-term effects.

1. Motivations Behind Demonetization

The rationale for demonetization was multi-faceted, with the government citing several key objectives:

- **Combating Black Money:** One of the primary aims was to curb the rampant black money circulating in the economy. The government argued that a significant portion of black money was hoarded in the form of high-denomination currency notes, and by invalidating these notes, it would force individuals to deposit their unaccounted wealth into the banking system.

- **Counterfeit Currency:** Another motivation was to tackle the issue of counterfeit currency, which had been used to fund terrorism and illegal activities. By eliminating high-value notes, the government aimed to reduce the circulation of fake currency.

- **Promoting Digital Transactions:** The move was also positioned as a step towards a cashless economy, encouraging citizens to adopt digital payment methods. This was expected to enhance transparency and traceability in financial transactions, further curbing corruption.

- **Enhancing Tax Compliance:** The government hoped that by formalizing a larger portion of the economy, tax compliance would improve. As more transactions moved through formal channels, it was anticipated that tax revenues would increase.

2. Execution of Demonetization

The execution of demonetization was marked by significant challenges:

- **Sudden Announcement:** The announcement was made with little prior notice, leaving citizens with a limited window to exchange their old notes for new ones. This abruptness led to widespread confusion and panic, as people rushed to banks and ATMs.
- **Logistical Challenges:** The demonetization process required the swift printing and distribution of new ₹500 and ₹2,000 notes. However, the limited availability of new currency initially created cash shortages across the country. Banks and ATMs were unprepared for the sudden demand, leading to long queues and frustration among the public.
- **Impact on Daily Life:** The sudden removal of high-denomination currency notes disrupted daily life and economic activities, particularly for those who relied heavily on cash transactions. Small businesses, daily wage workers, and rural populations faced acute hardships due to the cash crunch.

3. Immediate Impacts on the Economy

The immediate aftermath of demonetization had profound effects on various sectors of the economy:

- **Slowdown in Economic Growth:** Economic growth rates slowed in the months following demonetization. Sectors such as agriculture, construction, and retail, which were largely dependent on cash transactions, experienced significant declines in activity. The GDP growth rate fell, raising concerns about the overall health of the economy.
- **Job Losses:** Many businesses, especially in the informal sector, faced difficulties in managing cash flows. The cash crunch led to job losses, as companies were forced to downsize or shut down

operations. Migrant workers and daily wage earners were particularly affected, leading to widespread distress.

- **Rise of Digital Payments:** Despite the initial chaos, the demonetization drive did lead to a surge in digital payment adoption. Mobile wallets, online banking, and digital payment platforms gained popularity as consumers sought alternatives to cash transactions. This shift contributed to a gradual increase in financial inclusion and access to banking services.

4. Long-Term Effects and Ongoing Debates

The long-term effects of demonetization continue to be debated among economists, policymakers, and the public:

- **Success in Black Money Recovery:** While the government claimed that demonetization helped uncover a significant amount of black money, critics argued that the actual recovery was minimal compared to the total estimated black money in circulation. Many individuals found ways to convert their unaccounted wealth into other forms or through loopholes, limiting the effectiveness of the initiative.
- **Impact on Formalization of the Economy:** Proponents of demonetization argue that the move facilitated a shift towards a more formalized economy, encouraging greater tax compliance and enhancing government revenue. However, critics contend that the burden of transitioning to a cashless system disproportionately affected the lower-income population, who were less prepared for such a rapid change.
- **Evaluation of Economic Strategy:** The demonetization experiment prompted a reevaluation of India's broader economic strategy. Many questioned whether the decision was a politically motivated move rather than a well-planned economic reform. The long-term impact on public trust in the government and its economic policies remains to be seen.

A Mixed Legacy

Demonetization was a bold and unprecedented step in India's economic history, aiming to address deep-rooted issues such as black money, corruption, and counterfeit currency. While it led to some positive shifts, particularly in digital payments, the immediate disruptions and economic slowdown raised critical questions about the effectiveness of such a drastic policy.

As India continues to grapple with the challenges of a rapidly evolving economy, the lessons learned from demonetization will be essential in shaping future economic policies and reforms. Ultimately, the success of demonetization will be judged not just by its immediate outcomes, but by its long-term impact on India's financial landscape and its ability to foster a more transparent and equitable economy.

Farm Bills: Reforming Agricultural Policies

In September 2020, the Government of India introduced three contentious Farm Bills aimed at transforming the agricultural landscape of the country. These bills were seen as a critical step toward modernizing agriculture, improving farmers' incomes, and integrating the agricultural market with the broader economy. However, the introduction of these bills sparked significant controversy and widespread protests, leading to a national debate about the future of agriculture in India. This section explores the objectives behind the Farm Bills, their provisions, the farmers' response, and the broader implications for the agricultural sector.

1. Objectives Behind the Farm Bills

The primary objectives of the Farm Bills were to enhance farmers' autonomy, boost their income, and encourage investment in the agriculture sector. The government positioned these bills as a means to achieve several goals:

- **Market Freedom:** The bills aimed to provide farmers with greater freedom to sell their produce outside the traditional

Agricultural Produce Market Committee (APMC) mandis. This was expected to enhance competition and give farmers more options for selling their crops.

- **Improved Pricing Mechanisms:** The government sought to facilitate a system where farmers could negotiate prices directly with buyers, thereby reducing the influence of middlemen and allowing farmers to receive a fairer share of the market price.

- **Promotion of Contract Farming:** One of the key provisions of the bills was to promote contract farming, enabling farmers to enter into agreements with buyers before the sowing season. This was intended to ensure that farmers would have assured markets for their produce, thereby reducing risks associated with price fluctuations.

- **Increased Private Investment:** By deregulating the agricultural market, the government aimed to attract private investment in agriculture, which was expected to lead to better infrastructure, technology, and innovation in farming practices.

2. Key Provisions of the Farm Bills

The three Farm Bills introduced in 2020 were:

- **The Farmers' Produce Trade and Commerce (Promotion and Facilitation) Act, 2020:** This bill aimed to create a national market for agricultural produce by allowing farmers to sell their produce directly to buyers outside the APMC mandis. It sought to eliminate state-imposed barriers and fees associated with selling in these markets.

- **The Farmers (Empowerment and Protection) Agreement on Price Assurance and Farm Services Act, 2020:** This legislation focused on promoting contract farming. It established a framework for farmers to enter into contracts with buyers, outlining terms of sale, price guarantees, and dispute resolution mechanisms.

- **The Essential Commodities (Amendment) Act, 2020:** This bill sought to deregulate the production, supply, and distribution of certain agricultural commodities. It aimed to remove restrictions on stock limits and enhance the flow of goods in the market, thereby ensuring that farmers could sell their produce without undue constraints.

3. Farmers' Response and Protests

Despite the government's assurances about the benefits of the Farm Bills, they faced immense backlash from farmers, particularly from Punjab and Haryana. The protests, which began in late 2020, quickly spread across the country, leading to a large-scale mobilization of farmers, agricultural workers, and supporters.

- **Concerns Over MSP:** A major point of contention was the lack of legal guarantees for the Minimum Support Price (MSP). Farmers feared that the deregulation of markets would lead to the exploitation of their produce and threaten their livelihoods, as private buyers could potentially offer lower prices than the MSP.
- **Fear of Corporate Exploitation:** Many farmers expressed concerns that the Farm Bills would pave the way for increased corporate control over agriculture, undermining their bargaining power and leading to a system where small farmers would be at the mercy of large corporations.
- **Rejection of Government Dialogue:** The government's attempts to negotiate and address farmers' concerns were met with skepticism. Farmers demanded the repeal of the Farm Bills and organized nationwide protests, including sit-ins at key locations like the Delhi border.

4. Implications for Agriculture and the Economy

The Farm Bills and the subsequent protests brought to the forefront critical issues regarding the future of agriculture in India:

- **Need for Comprehensive Reform:** The protests highlighted the need for a holistic approach to agricultural reform, one that addresses the myriad challenges faced by farmers, including access to credit, technology, and insurance.
- **Dialogue and Consensus:** The unrest underscored the importance of involving farmers in the policymaking process. For any agricultural reform to succeed, it must be built on a foundation of trust and collaboration between the government and farmers.
- **Long-term Vision for Agriculture:** The debate surrounding the Farm Bills calls for a long-term vision for Indian agriculture that balances modernization with the protection of farmers' rights and livelihoods. Sustainable agricultural practices, fair pricing mechanisms, and investment in rural infrastructure are crucial to achieving this balance.

Navigating Agricultural Change

The introduction of the Farm Bills marked a significant attempt at reforming agricultural policies in India. While the government's objectives were aimed at modernizing the sector and improving farmers' incomes, the backlash from farmers emphasized the complexities of implementing such changes.

The ongoing debate surrounding these bills serves as a reminder that successful agricultural reform requires not only sound policy decisions but also the active engagement and consent of the farming community. Moving forward, it is essential to foster dialogue, build trust, and create policies that genuinely support farmers while embracing the realities of a rapidly changing agricultural landscape. As India continues to navigate the challenges of agricultural reform, the lessons learned from the Farm Bills will be pivotal in shaping a more sustainable and equitable future for the nation's farmers.

Role of Civil Society and Grassroots Movements

In the landscape of Indian politics, civil society and grassroots movements play a pivotal role in shaping public discourse, advocating for social justice, and pushing for political change. As the country grapples with various issues such as economic reforms, social inequalities, and environmental challenges, the contributions of civil society organizations (CSOs) and grassroots movements become increasingly vital. This section delves into the significance of these entities, their methods of operation, and their impact on the political landscape, especially in the context of major political changes like economic liberalization, demonetization, and agricultural reforms.

1. Understanding Civil Society and Grassroots Movements

Civil Society: Civil society refers to the arena of organized social life that is voluntary, self-generating, and autonomous from the state. It encompasses non-governmental organizations (NGOs), community-based organizations, advocacy groups, and social movements. These entities operate independently of government control and often serve as intermediaries between the state and the public. Their objectives typically include promoting human rights, advocating for policy reforms, and holding the government accountable.

Grassroots Movements: Grassroots movements are initiatives that emerge from the local level, mobilizing ordinary citizens to advocate for change. These movements often address specific issues affecting communities, such as environmental degradation, social injustice, or economic inequalities. Grassroots movements are characterized by their emphasis on local participation, collective action, and community empowerment.

2. Historical Context of Civil Society in India

The roots of civil society in India can be traced back to the freedom struggle, where various social reformers and movements fought against colonial rule. Leaders like Mahatma Gandhi emphasized the importance of collective action and grassroots mobilization. Post-independence, civil society organizations have evolved to address a wide range of issues, including poverty alleviation, education, health care, and environmental sustainability. The liberalization of the economy in the 1990s also led to the proliferation of NGOs, as the space for civil society expanded.

3. The Role of Civil Society in Political Change

Civil society organizations have been instrumental in advocating for political change through various mechanisms:

- **Advocacy and Lobbying:** CSOs engage in advocacy efforts to influence policymakers and legislators. They conduct research, organize campaigns, and mobilize public opinion to promote specific policy changes. For instance, during the economic liberalization era, organizations focused on the rights of marginalized communities, ensuring that their voices were heard in discussions about market reforms.
- **Raising Awareness:** Civil society plays a crucial role in educating citizens about their rights and responsibilities. Through campaigns, workshops, and community outreach, organizations raise awareness about social issues, empowering individuals to participate in the political process.
- **Accountability and Transparency:** CSOs often act as watchdogs, holding governments accountable for their actions. They monitor the implementation of policies, expose corruption, and advocate for transparency in governance. This function is particularly significant in a democratic setup, where public scrutiny is essential for good governance.

4. Grassroots Movements and Their Impact

Grassroots movements have been pivotal in mobilizing citizens around specific causes and demands:

- **Collective Action:** Movements like the Narmada Bachao Andolan (NBA) and the anti-CAA protests showcased the power of collective action in challenging government policies. These movements brought together diverse groups of people, emphasizing solidarity and shared goals, thereby amplifying their voices in the political arena.

- **Challenging Dominant Narratives:** Grassroots movements often challenge the dominant political narratives by highlighting the issues faced by marginalized communities. For example, movements focused on tribal rights and land acquisition have exposed the adverse effects of development projects on indigenous populations, demanding recognition and justice.
- **Building Networks:** Grassroots movements frequently build networks of solidarity among different communities, fostering a sense of unity in diversity. This interconnectedness enhances their capacity to challenge injustices and advocate for change more effectively.

5. Civil Society in the Context of Recent Political Changes

The role of civil society and grassroots movements has been particularly pronounced during significant political changes:

- **Economic Liberalization:** Following the liberalization policies of the 1990s, civil society organizations began advocating for the rights of the disadvantaged, emphasizing the need for inclusive growth. They pushed for policies that addressed the socio-economic disparities that emerged as a result of market-driven reforms.
- **Demonetization:** The abrupt demonetization in 2016 drew widespread criticism from civil society groups, who argued that it disproportionately affected the poor and marginalized. Activists organized protests, disseminated information, and highlighted the negative impacts of demonetization on livelihoods and the informal economy.
- **Farm Bills and Agricultural Reforms:** The protests against the Farm Bills in 2020 saw a significant mobilization of civil society and grassroots movements. Organizations worked alongside farmers to amplify their demands, advocate for their rights,

and challenge the government's narrative regarding the reforms.

6. Challenges Faced by Civil Society and Grassroots Movements

Despite their critical role, civil society organizations and grassroots movements face numerous challenges:

- **Repressive Measures:** In recent years, there has been a growing trend of state repression against civil society organizations. Many NGOs have faced restrictions on funding, censorship, and legal challenges, which hinder their ability to operate effectively.
- **Fragmentation:** The vast landscape of civil society is often fragmented, with multiple organizations working on similar issues without coordination. This fragmentation can dilute their collective impact and hinder concerted efforts for change.
- **Sustainability:** Many grassroots movements struggle with sustainability due to a lack of resources, funding, and organizational capacity. This challenge limits their ability to maintain momentum and achieve long-term goals.

The Future of Civil Society and Grassroots Movements

The role of civil society and grassroots movements in shaping Indian politics cannot be overstated. As the country continues to navigate complex political and social issues, these entities will remain essential in advocating for change, holding the government accountable, and empowering citizens.

Moving forward, fostering a conducive environment for civil society organizations and grassroots movements will be crucial for promoting democratic values and ensuring that the voices of marginalized communities are heard. By building coalitions, enhancing capacity, and advocating for their rights, civil society can play a transformative role in shaping a more equitable and just society. As

India progresses into the future, the synergy between political change and civil society engagement will be vital in addressing the challenges facing the nation and ensuring sustainable development for all.

Conclusion

The Politics of Change in India is a complex and dynamic arena, marked by a series of transformative events that have reshaped the socio-economic landscape of the country. As we navigate through the implications of significant political decisions—such as economic liberalization, demonetization, and the introduction of controversial farm bills—it becomes increasingly clear that these actions are not merely economic measures but also deeply political choices that have far-reaching consequences.

1. Interconnectedness of Economic and Political Changes

The relationship between politics and economics in India is profoundly interconnected. Economic policies are often reflective of the political ideologies and priorities of the ruling government, and they can significantly impact the lives of ordinary citizens. The economic liberalization initiated in the 1990s, for instance, opened India to global markets and has led to unprecedented growth, but it has also exacerbated inequalities and left many behind. Similarly, demonetization aimed to curb black money and counterfeit currency but resulted in severe disruptions to the cash-dependent economy, affecting millions of livelihoods.

The introduction of farm bills aimed at reforming agricultural policies generated significant unrest among farmers, demonstrating how political decisions can incite mass mobilization and dissent. These events highlight the critical need for a nuanced understanding of the implications of political choices, not only for economic growth but also for social stability and equity.

2. The Role of Civil Society in Driving Change

Civil society and grassroots movements have emerged as powerful agents of change in this political landscape. Their advocacy for accountability, transparency, and social justice has played a crucial role in shaping public policy and holding the government accountable. The ability of these organizations to mobilize citizens around specific issues, such as economic reform or environmental sustainability, underscores their importance in a democratic society.

Moreover, the active participation of citizens in movements, protests, and advocacy efforts has become a defining feature of contemporary Indian politics. This engagement reflects a growing awareness among the populace about their rights and responsibilities, as well as a desire to influence the direction of national policies.

3. Looking Ahead: Navigating Future Challenges

As India moves forward, it faces several challenges that require thoughtful political engagement and reform. The economic disparities highlighted by recent policies must be addressed to ensure that growth is inclusive and equitable. This includes recognizing the needs of marginalized communities and ensuring their voices are heard in the political process.

Furthermore, the need for effective governance that prioritizes transparency and accountability is paramount. Initiatives to combat corruption, ensure fair distribution of resources, and create a more inclusive political environment will be essential for fostering public trust and confidence in government institutions.

4. A Call for Informed Engagement

In conclusion, the Politics of Change in India underscores the significance of being informed and engaged citizens. Understanding the intricacies of political decisions and their implications is crucial for all stakeholders, including young people, educators, and civil society organizations. By fostering a culture of informed engagement, we can better navigate the complexities of Indian politics and advocate for meaningful change.

As we reflect on the lessons learned from past political decisions and their consequences, it is imperative to remain vigilant and proactive in shaping the future of our democracy. By embracing the principles of transparency, accountability, and inclusivity, we can work collectively toward a more just and equitable society for all. The journey ahead may be challenging, but the potential for positive change is immense, and it rests in the hands of an informed and engaged citizenry.

PART IV: POLITICS AND ECONOMY

| 11 |

Political Influence on the Indian Economy

Politics and economic policies in India have a symbiotic relationship, where governmental decisions and reforms significantly impact economic growth, industrial development, and investor confidence. This chapter explores the influence of politics on the Indian economy, examining key economic policies, reforms, political stability's impact on foreign direct investment (FDI), and the dynamics between the public and private sectors.

Economic Policies and Reforms

Economic policies and reforms are central to understanding the political landscape of India. They not only reflect the government's approach to economic management but also embody the ideological beliefs of political leaders and parties. This section explores the major economic policies and reforms that have significantly shaped India's economy since independence, highlighting the intersection of politics and economics.

1. The Era of Planned Economy (1947–1991)

Upon gaining independence in 1947, India adopted a mixed economy model, combining elements of socialism and capitalism. The government took a dominant role in economic planning and management through the establishment of five-year plans. The focus during this period was on self-sufficiency, industrialization, and social welfare. Major industries were nationalized, and extensive regulations were introduced to control the economy.

While these policies aimed to reduce inequality and stimulate growth, they often led to inefficiencies, bureaucratic red tape, and corruption. The economy remained largely closed to global markets, resulting in stagnation and limited technological advancement.

2. Economic Liberalization (1991)

The watershed moment for India's economy came in 1991 when the country faced a severe balance of payments crisis. The government, led by then-Finance Minister Manmohan Singh, initiated a series of sweeping economic reforms that marked a shift from a state-controlled to a market-oriented economy. Key elements of these reforms included:

- **Deregulation:** The removal of various industrial licensing requirements aimed to encourage entrepreneurship and investment.
- **Privatization:** The government began disinvesting its stake in public sector enterprises, promoting private ownership and management.
- **Opening Up to Foreign Investment:** Policies were introduced to attract foreign direct investment (FDI) by relaxing restrictions and improving the ease of doing business.
- **Trade Liberalization:** Tariffs were reduced, and import restrictions were lifted, allowing for greater competition and access to global markets.

These reforms catalyzed rapid economic growth, transforming India into one of the world's fastest-growing economies. They led to significant increases in GDP, urbanization, and improvements in living standards for many. However, the benefits were not uniformly distributed, leading to increased inequalities and regional disparities.

3. The Green Revolution (1960s-1980s)

The Green Revolution was a significant agricultural reform initiative aimed at increasing food production to combat hunger and poverty. By introducing high-yield variety (HYV) seeds, chemical fertilizers, and advanced irrigation techniques, the government sought to modernize agriculture. This initiative was politically motivated, as ensuring food security was crucial for the legitimacy of the government.

The success of the Green Revolution transformed India from a food-deficient country to one of self-sufficiency in food grain production. However, it also led to environmental degradation, increased debt among farmers, and socio-economic disparities in rural areas.

4. Goods and Services Tax (GST) (2017)

The introduction of the Goods and Services Tax (GST) in 2017 represented a landmark reform in India's indirect tax system. This policy aimed to create a unified market by subsuming multiple indirect taxes into a single tax regime, thereby simplifying the tax structure and increasing compliance.

The GST was politically contentious, with debates over its implementation and rates. Nevertheless, it has streamlined tax administration, reduced tax evasion, and improved revenue collection for the government. The reform reflects the political imperative to enhance economic efficiency while addressing the challenges of a complex federal structure.

5. Demonetization (2016)

In November 2016, Prime Minister Narendra Modi announced the demonetization of ◈500 and ◈1,000 currency notes as a measure to combat black money, counterfeit currency, and corruption. This sudden decision aimed to formalize the economy and encourage digital transactions.

While the intent was to enhance transparency in the economy, the implementation faced significant criticism. The abrupt withdrawal of cash led to widespread disruptions, affecting small businesses and daily wage workers. The long-term benefits of demonetization remain debated, highlighting the political risks associated with drastic economic policies.

6. Recent Reforms and Initiatives

In recent years, various initiatives have emerged that reflect the government's focus on economic growth, employment generation, and technological advancement. These include:

- **Make in India:** Launched in 2014, this initiative aims to boost manufacturing by attracting investment and creating job opportunities. It reflects a political vision to position India as a global manufacturing hub.
- **Digital India:** This campaign promotes digital infrastructure and aims to enhance digital literacy and access to technology. It underscores the political drive toward modernization and innovation.
- **Atmanirbhar Bharat (Self-Reliant India):** Announced during the COVID-19 pandemic, this initiative seeks to promote self-reliance in various sectors, from agriculture to manufacturing, by reducing dependency on imports. The political narrative focuses on resilience and sustainability in the face of global challenges.

The evolution of economic policies and reforms in India reflects the intricate relationship between politics and the economy. Each significant policy shift has been shaped by political motivations, social imperatives, and economic realities. As India continues to navigate the complexities of a rapidly changing global landscape, the political will to implement effective economic reforms will be crucial for sustaining growth, addressing inequalities, and ensuring a more equitable future for all citizens. Understanding this dynamic is essential for grasping the broader implications of political decisions on the nation's economy and the well-being of its people.

Political Stability and Foreign Investment

Political stability is a crucial factor that significantly influences foreign investment decisions in any country. For investors, stability provides a sense of security, predictability, and confidence in the economic environment. In the context of India, the relationship between political stability and foreign direct investment (FDI) has evolved over the years, reflecting the broader socio-economic and political dynamics of the nation. This section delves into the importance of political stability for foreign investment in India, examining its historical context, current trends, and future implications.

1. Understanding Foreign Direct Investment (FDI)

Foreign Direct Investment (FDI) refers to investments made by foreign entities in domestic businesses, typically involving significant ownership and control over the invested enterprise. FDI is vital for a country's economic growth as it brings in capital, technology, management expertise, and access to international markets. For countries like India, attracting FDI is essential for stimulating economic development, creating jobs, and enhancing competitiveness.

2. The Role of Political Stability in FDI Decisions

Political stability plays a multifaceted role in influencing FDI decisions:

- **Risk Mitigation:** Investors seek to minimize risks associated with their investments. Political instability—characterized by frequent changes in government, civil unrest, or social tensions—can lead to unpredictable policy shifts and regulatory challenges. A stable political environment mitigates these risks, making the investment landscape more appealing.

- **Predictable Policy Framework:** Political stability often results in a consistent and predictable policy framework. This is crucial for long-term investments as businesses require assurance that policies will not change abruptly, affecting their operational viability and profitability.

- **Infrastructure Development:** Stable political conditions enable governments to plan and implement infrastructure projects effectively. Good infrastructure, including transport, power, and communication networks, is vital for attracting and sustaining FDI, as it reduces operational costs for businesses.
- **Improved Regulatory Environment:** A stable political climate fosters a conducive regulatory environment that promotes ease of doing business. Investors are more likely to engage with a country where regulations are clear, transparent, and enforced consistently.

3. Historical Context: FDI in India

Historically, India has experienced varying degrees of political stability, which has impacted its FDI landscape:

- **Pre-Liberalization Era (1947-1991):** Post-independence, India adopted a mixed economy model, characterized by significant government intervention and control. During this period, FDI was limited, and political instability—stemming from regional tensions, social unrest, and frequent changes in government—resulted in a lack of investor confidence.
- **Economic Liberalization (1991):** The 1991 economic reforms marked a turning point for India's FDI landscape. The liberalization process coincided with a period of relative political stability under the leadership of the Congress party. As the government opened up the economy, it established a more favorable environment for foreign investment, leading to a significant increase in FDI inflows.
- **Subsequent Decades:** The political stability experienced in the 2000s, particularly during the tenure of the United Progressive Alliance (UPA) government, facilitated robust FDI growth. However, instances of political instability, such as the political turmoil during the UPA's second term and the challenges faced

by the National Democratic Alliance (NDA) government in its early years, impacted investor sentiment temporarily.

4. Current Trends in Political Stability and FDI

In recent years, India has witnessed significant changes in its political landscape, which have implications for FDI:

- **Strong Government Mandate:** The electoral victories of the NDA government under Prime Minister Narendra Modi in 2014 and 2019 provided a strong mandate for reform. The government's commitment to economic reforms and infrastructure development has bolstered investor confidence, leading to increased FDI inflows.
- **Focus on 'Make in India':** Initiatives like 'Make in India' aim to promote manufacturing and attract FDI by creating a conducive business environment. The government's political will to enhance ease of doing business has further reinforced stability, making India an attractive destination for foreign investors.
- **Global Challenges:** Global challenges, including the COVID-19 pandemic and geopolitical tensions, have reshaped the FDI landscape. India's political stability during these turbulent times has positioned it as a reliable alternative for companies looking to diversify their supply chains and operations.

5. The Impact of Political Instability on FDI

While political stability attracts FDI, political instability can have detrimental effects:

- **Investment Withdrawals:** Instances of political upheaval, policy reversals, or civil unrest can lead to immediate withdrawal or reduction of foreign investments. Companies may fear disruptions to their operations, leading them to reallocate resources to more stable environments.

- **Delayed Investments:** Uncertainty surrounding political developments can result in delayed investment decisions. Potential investors may adopt a wait-and-see approach, holding back on commitments until they perceive a more stable environment.
- **Reputational Risks:** Political instability can damage a country's reputation as an investment destination. Negative media coverage, concerns over governance, and perceptions of risk can deter foreign investors.

6. Future Outlook: Political Stability and FDI in India

As India continues to navigate the complexities of a dynamic political landscape, the interplay between political stability and FDI will remain pivotal:

- **Strengthening Institutions:** Enhancing the robustness of democratic institutions, promoting transparency, and ensuring the rule of law will contribute to political stability and bolster investor confidence.
- **Long-term Vision:** A consistent and long-term vision for economic growth, supported by stable political leadership, will be crucial in sustaining FDI inflows. Addressing structural challenges and ensuring inclusive growth will further enhance India's attractiveness to foreign investors.
- **Engaging with Global Trends:** As geopolitical dynamics shift, India must position itself as a reliable partner for global investors. Building strong international relationships and ensuring political stability will be key in attracting foreign investment.

Political stability is a cornerstone of foreign investment in India, shaping the nation's economic trajectory. By fostering a predictable and secure environment, India can continue to attract FDI that drives growth, innovation, and development. As the country embraces its potential in the global economy, the interplay between political stability and economic reform will be instrumental in determining its success in the years to come. Understanding this relationship is essential for policymakers, investors, and citizens alike as they navigate the complexities of India's political economy.

Public Sector vs. Private Sector: The Political Influence on Industries

The relationship between the public and private sectors is a fundamental aspect of any economy, including India's. Both sectors play pivotal roles in driving economic growth, job creation, and development. However, political decisions heavily influence how these sectors operate, their priorities, and their contributions to the economy. This section examines the dynamics between the public and private sectors in India, exploring their roles in key industries such as coal, telecom, and aviation, as well as the impact of political decisions on their functioning.

1. Defining the Public and Private Sectors

- **Public Sector:** The public sector encompasses government-owned enterprises and institutions that provide essential services and goods. These entities operate under government control, aiming to serve public interests rather than maximize profits. Key industries within the public sector include utilities, transportation, healthcare, and education.
- **Private Sector:** The private sector consists of businesses owned and operated by private individuals or corporations. These enterprises aim to generate profits and contribute to economic growth. The private sector encompasses a wide range of industries, including manufacturing, services, technology, and finance.

2. Political Influence on the Public Sector

The public sector in India has historically been shaped by political decisions and ideologies. The government plays a significant role in determining the structure, functioning, and funding of public enterprises. Key points of influence include:

- **Policy Framework:** Political parties and governments set the policy framework within which public sector enterprises operate. These policies can affect everything from operational guidelines to funding allocations, often reflecting the ruling party's ideological stance. For instance, a government prioritizing social welfare may increase funding for public healthcare, while one focused on economic growth may push for privatization.
- **Appointment and Accountability:** Political considerations often influence appointments in public sector enterprises. Political parties may appoint individuals based on loyalty or connections rather than merit, impacting the efficiency and accountability of these enterprises. This can lead to issues such as corruption, inefficiency, and a lack of transparency.
- **Public Sector Reforms:** The political climate often determines the pace and nature of public sector reforms. For example, the liberalization of the Indian economy in the 1990s was driven by political decisions to open up the economy, leading to significant reforms in the public sector. However, resistance from certain political factions can slow down necessary reforms.

3. Political Influence on the Private Sector

While the private sector is primarily driven by market forces, political decisions can significantly impact its growth and operations. This influence manifests in several ways:

- **Regulatory Environment:** The regulatory framework set by the government can either facilitate or hinder private sector growth. For instance, complex regulations, licensing requirements, and bureaucratic hurdles can stifle entrepreneurship and innovation. Conversely, a favorable regulatory environment can encourage investment and expansion.

- **Tax Policies:** Tax policies, including incentives and subsidies, can influence private sector decisions regarding investments and operations. Governments may introduce tax breaks to attract foreign investment or stimulate certain industries, which can have lasting effects on the economy.

- **Public-Private Partnerships (PPPs):** Political decisions often drive the establishment of public-private partnerships, which leverage private sector efficiency and investment in public services and infrastructure. Successful PPPs can lead to improved service delivery, but failures can occur if political motivations overshadow practical considerations.

4. Key Industries: Coal, Telecom, and Aviation

- **Coal Industry:** The coal industry in India is predominantly public sector-driven, with the Coal India Limited (CIL) being the largest producer. Political decisions regarding coal allocations, environmental regulations, and pricing mechanisms significantly impact this sector. The push for privatization and competitive bidding has led to increased investments but also sparked controversies over environmental concerns and displacement issues.

- **Telecom Industry:** The telecommunications sector has witnessed significant transformation due to political decisions. The liberalization policies of the 1990s opened the market to private players, leading to rapid growth and competition. However, political influences have continued to shape the industry through regulatory frameworks, spectrum allocation, and pricing policies, impacting both service providers and consumers.

- **Aviation Industry:** The aviation sector in India has seen substantial growth, influenced by both public and private sector dynamics. The privatization of airports and the entry of private airlines have transformed the industry. Political decisions regarding air traffic rights, international partnerships, and safety regulations continue to play a crucial role in shaping the industry's future.

5. Challenges and Opportunities

The interplay between the public and private sectors in India presents both challenges and opportunities:

- **Inefficiencies and Corruption:** The public sector often grapples with inefficiencies, bureaucratic red tape, and corruption. Political influences can exacerbate these issues, impacting service delivery and public trust.
- **Need for Collaboration:** Strengthening collaboration between the public and private sectors can enhance service delivery and infrastructure development. Effective public-private partnerships can leverage the strengths of both sectors, fostering innovation and efficiency.
- **Role of Technology:** Advancements in technology can bridge gaps between the public and private sectors. The use of digital platforms can enhance transparency, improve service delivery, and create a more competitive environment.

6. Future Outlook

Looking ahead, the relationship between the public and private sectors will continue to evolve:

- **Balancing Interests:** As India progresses, balancing the interests of the public and private sectors will be crucial. Policymakers must ensure that public enterprises remain efficient and accountable while creating a conducive environment for private investment.

- **Focus on Sustainability:** Future political decisions should prioritize sustainability and social responsibility in both sectors. Addressing environmental concerns and ensuring equitable growth will be essential for long-term stability.
- **Strengthening Institutions:** Robust institutions that promote accountability and transparency are vital for fostering a healthy relationship between the public and private sectors. Political will and effective governance will play a crucial role in achieving this goal.

The interplay between the public and private sectors is a defining characteristic of India's political economy. Political decisions shape the structure and functioning of both sectors, influencing their contributions to economic growth and development. As India navigates the complexities of its economic landscape, fostering collaboration and accountability between these sectors will be essential for realizing the nation's potential and ensuring inclusive growth. Understanding this dynamic is crucial for policymakers, investors, and citizens alike as they engage with the evolving political and economic landscape of India.

Conclusion: The Interplay of Politics and Economy in India

The intricate relationship between politics and the economy is a defining characteristic of India's developmental journey. As explored throughout this chapter, political decisions shape the landscape of economic policies and reforms, influencing everything from foreign direct investment to the operational dynamics of public and private sectors. Understanding this interplay is crucial for grasping how India's economy has evolved and the challenges it faces moving forward.

1. Historical Context and Its Impact

India's economic trajectory cannot be divorced from its political history. The colonial legacy established a governance framework that has influenced contemporary policies. Post-independence, the government adopted a mixed economy model, balancing between public ownership and private enterprise. Major reforms, such as the Green Revolution, liberalization in the 1990s, and recent initiatives like the Goods and Services Tax (GST), have been significant in reshaping the economy. However, these reforms have also faced challenges, including political resistance, bureaucratic hurdles, and the need for continuous adaptation to global trends.

2. Challenges in Political Decision-Making

Political instability and shifts in power dynamics can disrupt economic planning and execution. Decisions influenced by electoral politics often prioritize short-term gains over long-term economic stability. The impact of such decisions can be seen in instances like demonetization, where abrupt changes in policy had immediate repercussions on the economy, affecting various sectors and the informal economy significantly.

3. Foreign Investment and Political Stability

Political stability is a prerequisite for attracting foreign direct investment (FDI). Investors seek a predictable and conducive environment for their operations. In this context, India has made significant strides, particularly since the 1991 liberalization. However, fluctuations in political support for economic policies can lead to uncertainties. Ensuring a consistent and transparent policy framework is essential for maintaining investor confidence and fostering sustainable economic growth.

4. The Dichotomy of Public and Private Sectors

The dynamics between the public and private sectors remain complex and often contentious. While the public sector is crucial for providing essential services and infrastructure, the private sector is the engine of innovation and efficiency. The political landscape influences the balance between these sectors, determining how resources are allocated and how policies are formulated. As the government continues to explore privatization and public-private partnerships, it must ensure that these moves do not compromise public welfare or lead to monopolistic practices.

5. Looking Ahead: The Need for Reform and Adaptation

As India stands at a crossroads, the need for further reforms becomes evident. The future of the Indian economy hinges on the ability to adapt to changing global dynamics, technological advancements, and domestic challenges such as income inequality and unemployment. Policymakers must be proactive in crafting strategies that promote inclusive growth while addressing systemic issues like corruption and bureaucratic inefficiencies.

6. The Role of Civil Society and Public Engagement

The role of civil society in shaping economic policies is becoming increasingly significant. Grassroots movements and public engagement can provide valuable insights and push for reforms that align with the needs of the populace. Political leaders must recognize the importance of dialogue and collaboration with civil society to foster policies that are not only economically sound but also socially just.

Final Thoughts

In conclusion, the political influence on the Indian economy is multifaceted and deeply intertwined with the country's history and societal structures. As India continues to navigate its path toward becoming a global economic powerhouse, understanding and addressing the political dimensions of economic policies will be paramount. For students, educators, and policymakers, recognizing this interplay can lead to more informed decisions that not only enhance economic growth but also promote a more equitable and just society. The journey ahead requires a collective effort to harness the power of politics for the betterment of the economy, ensuring that it serves the interests of all citizens and sustains India's aspirations for a brighter future.

| **12** |

How Politics Shapes Jobs and Education

Politics plays a pivotal role in shaping both the job market and educational landscape in India. This chapter explores how political decisions influence employment opportunities, the effectiveness of job creation schemes, and the evolution of educational policies.

Unemployment and Political Promises

Unemployment remains one of the most pressing challenges in India, affecting millions of citizens and significantly influencing the country's social and economic fabric. The interplay between politics and unemployment is profound, as political parties often leverage the issue in their electoral strategies, making promises that can shape policy frameworks yet frequently fall short of tangible results. This section delves into how political promises are crafted in response to unemployment, the effectiveness of these commitments, and the broader implications for the labor market.

1. The Political Landscape of Unemployment

Unemployment is not merely an economic statistic; it is a critical political issue that impacts the electorate's mood and preferences. With a significant portion of the Indian population being young and aspirational, political parties often prioritize job creation in their manifestos, recognizing that the promise of employment can sway voters. The reliance on youth votes has led to the introduction of numerous schemes aimed at job creation, particularly during election cycles. However, the commitment to job creation can sometimes be more about gaining electoral advantage than addressing the underlying systemic issues that contribute to unemployment.

2. Key Political Promises and Their Implementation

Political parties frequently promise to generate jobs through various means, such as:

- **Skill Development Programs:** Governments often announce initiatives aimed at skill development and vocational training to equip the workforce with the necessary skills for emerging industries. The National Skill Development Mission is an example of such an initiative, aiming to create a skilled workforce to meet the demands of a growing economy. However, the implementation of these programs has been inconsistent, leading to skepticism about their effectiveness.
- **Make in India Initiative:** Launched in 2014, the Make in India initiative aimed to transform India into a global manufacturing hub. It was touted as a means to generate millions of jobs across various sectors. While the initiative did lead to some growth in manufacturing, the anticipated job creation did not materialize at the expected rate, leading to criticism regarding the effectiveness of the government's approach.
- **Employment Schemes:** Various employment generation schemes, such as the Mahatma Gandhi National Rural Employment Guarantee Act (MGNREGA), have been introduced to provide guaranteed workdays to rural households. While MGNREGA has succeeded in alleviating rural poverty and providing a safety net, concerns about wage rates and the sustainability of such programs persist.

3. The Disconnect Between Promises and Reality

Despite the political rhetoric surrounding job creation, the reality often reflects a significant disconnect. Several factors contribute to this gap:

- **Implementation Challenges:** Many job creation schemes face bureaucratic inefficiencies, corruption, and lack of proper monitoring. The disconnect between policy formulation and ground-level implementation leads to underutilization of resources and missed opportunities for job creation.
- **Economic Context:** The economic landscape plays a crucial role in the success of job creation efforts. Global economic downturns, shifts in market demands, and disruptions caused by crises such as the COVID-19 pandemic can severely impact job availability. Political promises often fail to account for these broader economic realities.
- **Mismatch of Skills:** The skills taught in training programs frequently do not align with industry requirements. As a result, even when job openings exist, a significant gap remains between what employers seek and the skills job seekers possess.

4. Political Accountability and the Need for Reforms

To tackle the issue of unemployment effectively, political parties must be held accountable for their promises. This accountability can be fostered through:

- **Transparency in Reporting:** Establishing mechanisms for tracking the progress of job creation schemes and providing regular updates to the public can enhance accountability. Transparent reporting can build trust and allow citizens to assess the effectiveness of government initiatives.
- **Stakeholder Engagement:** Involving industry stakeholders, educators, and civil society in the policy-making process can ensure that job creation initiatives are grounded in the realities

of the job market. This collaborative approach can help identify skills gaps and tailor programs accordingly.

- **Long-term Vision:** Political parties need to adopt a long-term perspective on job creation rather than relying solely on short-term promises. Sustainable job creation requires addressing structural issues within the economy, including enhancing infrastructure, investing in education, and promoting entrepreneurship.

Towards a Job-Centric Politics

In conclusion, the relationship between unemployment and political promises is a complex and multifaceted issue in India. While political parties utilize the promise of job creation as a powerful electoral tool, the effectiveness of these promises often remains questionable due to implementation challenges and economic realities. Moving forward, it is imperative for political leaders to prioritize genuine job creation initiatives that are transparent, accountable, and aligned with the needs of the labor market. By fostering a job-centric political landscape, India can work towards reducing unemployment and achieving sustainable economic growth, ultimately enhancing the quality of life for its citizens.

Political Decisions in Education

Education is one of the cornerstones of societal development, and in India, it is profoundly influenced by political decisions. From policy formulation to the implementation of educational programs, the government's role is pivotal in shaping the educational landscape. This section explores the impact of political decisions on education in India, highlighting key policies, reforms, and their implications for students, educators, and society at large.

1. Education Policies and Legislative Framework

The foundation of India's educational system is laid down through various policies and acts, shaped significantly by political agendas.

The **Right to Education Act (RTE)**, enacted in 2009, is a landmark legislation that guarantees free and compulsory education for children aged 6 to 14. This act reflects the political commitment to education as a fundamental right. However, its implementation has been uneven across states, influenced by local governance, resources, and political will.

The **National Education Policy (NEP) 2020** aims to overhaul the educational framework by introducing significant reforms, such as the promotion of multilingual education, vocational training, and the integration of technology in teaching. While these reforms have the potential to enhance educational quality and accessibility, their success largely depends on political backing, administrative efficiency, and adequate funding.

2. Reservations and Equity in Education

Political decisions around **reservations** in education have sparked considerable debate and controversy. The provision of quotas for Scheduled Castes (SC), Scheduled Tribes (ST), and Other Backward Classes (OBC) in educational institutions aims to promote social equity and uplift marginalized communities. However, the implementation of these reservations often leads to political maneuvering, as parties seek to gain electoral support from various communities.

The politicization of reservations can create divisions within society, where some groups feel aggrieved while others benefit. This dynamic underscores the need for thoughtful political discourse and policies that genuinely address educational disparities without exacerbating societal tensions.

3. The Politicization of Student Unions

Student unions play a crucial role in advocating for the rights and needs of students. However, political parties often seek to influence these unions for their own gain. The **politicization of student bodies**, particularly in prominent universities like Jawaharlal Nehru University (JNU), has led to intense ideological battles, impacting the educational environment.

These student movements can drive meaningful change by raising awareness on critical issues, such as **fee hikes, infrastructure deficits, and curriculum reforms**. However, the involvement of political parties can also lead to a focus on ideological conflicts rather than substantive educational improvements.

4. Impact of Policy Changes on Curriculum and Pedagogy

Political decisions have a direct impact on curriculum development and pedagogical approaches in schools and universities. For instance, changes in government can lead to shifts in curriculum focus, with emphasis placed on particular ideologies or historical narratives. The introduction of new textbooks or changes in examination systems are often politically motivated and can lead to confusion and resistance among educators and students.

Additionally, educational policies can determine the balance between **theoretical knowledge and practical skills** in the curriculum. Political priorities can influence whether the education system leans more toward rote learning or fosters critical thinking and problem-solving skills essential for the modern workforce.

5. Funding and Resource Allocation

Political decisions significantly influence the funding and resource allocation for education. The allocation of budgets to educational institutions can reflect the government's priorities, often swayed by political considerations. For example, increased funding during election years may be a strategy to gain favor with the electorate, while reduced allocations in subsequent years can lead to challenges in maintaining educational standards.

Moreover, the **inequality in funding** between urban and rural schools is a persistent issue. Political will is essential to address these disparities and ensure that all students, regardless of their geographical location, have access to quality education.

6. The Role of Non-Governmental Organizations (NGOs)

Political decisions also create an environment where NGOs can play a crucial role in education. With varying degrees of success, NGOs often step in to fill gaps left by the government, providing alternative education models, advocating for educational reforms, and supporting marginalized communities. The relationship between the government and NGOs can be collaborative or adversarial, depending on the political climate and the alignment of their goals.

The Need for Inclusive and Forward-Thinking Policies

In conclusion, political decisions in education shape the future of millions of students in India. The interplay between policy formulation, implementation, and the political environment is complex and often contentious. For India to achieve its educational goals, it is imperative that political leaders prioritize inclusive, equitable, and sustainable educational policies that transcend partisan interests.

By fostering collaboration among various stakeholders—governments, educators, students, and civil society—India can create an educational landscape that truly empowers its youth and drives national development. Moving forward, the challenge lies in ensuring that political decisions serve the best interests of all students, promoting not just literacy but holistic development that prepares them for the complexities of the modern world.

Challenges and Reforms

The intersection of politics, jobs, and education in India presents a complex landscape characterized by numerous challenges and the pressing need for reforms. As the country grapples with high unemployment rates and a rapidly evolving job market, political decisions play a crucial role in shaping the policies and strategies aimed at addressing these issues. This section delves into the key challenges facing India in the realms of employment and education, while also highlighting potential reforms that could pave the way for a more responsive and effective system.

1. Challenges in Employment Generation

High Unemployment Rates: Despite being one of the fastest-growing economies in the world, India struggles with high unemployment rates, particularly among youth. According to various reports, the youth unemployment rate has been significantly higher than the national average, reflecting a disconnect between education and job market demands. This mismatch raises questions about the efficacy of current educational programs in equipping students with the skills needed for the evolving job landscape.

Informal Employment: A significant portion of the Indian workforce is engaged in the informal sector, which lacks job security, benefits, and protections. The informal economy often fails to provide stable employment opportunities, leading to economic instability for many families. Political efforts to formalize employment and extend labor rights to informal workers are ongoing, but the challenge remains substantial.

Skill Gaps: The lack of alignment between educational outcomes and industry requirements results in skill gaps that hinder job creation. Many graduates find themselves unprepared for the workforce, with employers expressing frustration over the availability of qualified candidates. This challenge is exacerbated by outdated curricula and inadequate vocational training programs.

2. Political Promises vs. Ground Reality

Election Promises: Political parties frequently make grand promises regarding job creation and employment schemes during election campaigns. However, the implementation of these promises often falls short. Programs like "Make in India" and "Skill India" have faced criticism for not delivering the expected results. The gap between promises and reality leads to disillusionment among voters, especially youth, who feel let down by the political system.

Bureaucratic Hurdles: The bureaucratic processes involved in implementing employment-related schemes can be cumbersome and inefficient. Delays, lack of coordination among departments, and corruption can hinder the effectiveness of programs intended to generate jobs. Streamlining these processes through political will and administrative reforms is essential for success.

3. Challenges in Education Reform

Quality of Education: The quality of education remains a significant challenge in India. Many public schools face issues such as inadequate infrastructure, shortage of qualified teachers, and outdated teaching methods. Political decisions regarding budget allocations and educational priorities greatly influence the quality of education that students receive.

Access and Inequality: Disparities in access to quality education, particularly between urban and rural areas, pose another challenge. Marginalized communities often face barriers to education, including economic constraints, cultural factors, and inadequate infrastructure. Political action is required to address these inequities and ensure that all students have access to quality education.

Resistance to Change: Reforming educational policies often meets resistance from various stakeholders, including teachers, parents, and political groups. The introduction of new curricula or teaching methods may encounter pushback due to entrenched beliefs and practices. Building consensus and effectively communicating the need for change are essential for successful reforms.

4. Potential Reforms for a Better Future

Curriculum and Skill Development: Reforming the curriculum to align with industry needs is crucial for bridging the skill gap. Incorporating practical training, internships, and vocational courses into the education system can prepare students for real-world challenges. Collaborating with industries to develop skill development programs can enhance employability.

Promotion of Entrepreneurship: Encouraging entrepreneurship can be a powerful strategy for job creation. Political initiatives aimed at providing support for startups, such as access to funding, mentorship, and training, can empower young people to create their own employment opportunities. Programs that foster an entrepreneurial mindset in educational institutions can stimulate innovation and job creation.

Strengthening Public Employment Schemes: Enhancing the effectiveness of public employment schemes, such as the Mahatma

Gandhi National Rural Employment Guarantee Act (MGNREGA), is vital for providing immediate relief to unemployed individuals. Political commitment to ensuring timely payments, increasing job opportunities, and addressing grievances can improve the program's effectiveness.

Comprehensive Policy Framework: A holistic policy framework that integrates education, skill development, and employment generation is essential for addressing the interconnected challenges. Political leaders must work towards creating cohesive policies that align educational outcomes with job market demands while prioritizing inclusivity and accessibility.

The Path Forward

The challenges in the realms of employment and education in India are multifaceted and require concerted political efforts to address. By recognizing the importance of these issues and implementing effective reforms, policymakers can create a more responsive and inclusive system that empowers individuals and contributes to national development. Engaging with stakeholders, promoting transparency, and prioritizing quality education and job creation are key steps in navigating the complexities of this landscape. With a renewed focus on the intersection of politics, jobs, and education, India can move toward a future where every individual has the opportunity to thrive and contribute to the nation's growth.

Conclusion: Bridging the Gap Between Politics, Jobs, and Education

In conclusion, the intricate relationship between politics, jobs, and education in India underscores the need for a multifaceted approach to address the challenges facing the country. As we have explored throughout this chapter, the interplay of political decisions and policies significantly impacts employment opportunities and the quality of education available to citizens. While there are promising initiatives and programs aimed at addressing these issues, significant gaps remain that require urgent attention.

1. The Need for Integrated Policies

A critical takeaway from this discussion is the importance of integrated policies that align educational outcomes with labor market demands. The education system must evolve to equip students with the necessary skills and competencies required in an ever-changing job market. Policymakers should prioritize collaboration between educational institutions, industries, and government bodies to create a responsive framework that fosters skill development and employment generation.

2. Political Accountability and Transparency

Political accountability plays a vital role in ensuring that promises made by political parties regarding job creation and education reforms are not only fulfilled but are also effective. The public's demand for transparency in the implementation of employment schemes and educational reforms is essential for fostering trust in the political system. Engaging citizens in the decision-making process and encouraging feedback can enhance accountability and lead to more effective governance.

3. Addressing Systemic Inequalities

As highlighted, systemic inequalities in access to quality education and job opportunities remain significant hurdles in achieving equitable growth. Political action must prioritize marginalized communities, ensuring that they have equal access to educational resources and employment opportunities. This involves not only formulating inclusive policies but also actively addressing historical injustices that have perpetuated inequality.

4. Encouraging Youth Participation

The involvement of youth in political discourse, advocacy, and decision-making is crucial for driving change. Young people, as the future leaders and workforce of the nation, must be encouraged to participate actively in shaping policies that affect their lives. Political leaders should create platforms for youth engagement, enabling them to voice their concerns and contribute to solutions. Empowering young individuals with the knowledge and tools necessary for political participation can lead to more responsive governance.

5. The Role of Civil Society

Civil society organizations play an essential role in advocating for policies that enhance job creation and educational reforms. They serve as watchdogs, holding the government accountable for its promises while also providing valuable insights into the challenges faced by citizens. Collaboration between the government and civil society can facilitate the development of more effective and inclusive policies.

A Vision for the Future

Ultimately, the vision for the future must encompass a holistic understanding of the interconnectedness of politics, jobs, and education. By prioritizing quality education, addressing skill gaps, promoting entrepreneurship, and ensuring political accountability, India can create an environment that fosters economic growth and social mobility. A commitment to reforming the education system and generating sustainable employment opportunities will not only empower individuals but also contribute to the nation's overall development.

As we look ahead, it is imperative for all stakeholders—government, educators, civil society, and citizens—to work together toward creating a robust framework that supports job creation and enhances educational outcomes. With concerted efforts and a shared vision, India can overcome its challenges and harness the potential of its youth, paving the way for a prosperous and inclusive future.

| 13 |

The Politics of Welfare and Development

Politics in India is intricately woven with welfare schemes and development projects aimed at addressing socio-economic challenges and fostering infrastructural growth. This chapter explores the strategic implementation, political motivations, and societal impacts of key welfare schemes and development initiatives.

Welfare Schemes: Political Strategies Behind Social Safety Nets

Welfare schemes in India serve as critical instruments for poverty alleviation, social upliftment, and economic development. They represent the government's commitment to providing essential services and support to marginalized sections of society. However, beyond their social implications, welfare schemes are deeply intertwined with the political landscape. This section will delve into the various welfare schemes implemented in India, their political motivations, and their impact on society.

1. Overview of Welfare Schemes

Welfare schemes can be broadly categorized into several types, including employment schemes, health care initiatives, financial assistance programs, and educational support. These programs aim to improve the quality of life for disadvantaged groups, including women, children, Scheduled Castes (SCs), Scheduled Tribes (STs), and other marginalized communities.

Some of the most notable welfare schemes include:

- **Mahatma Gandhi National Rural Employment Guarantee Act (MGNREGA):** This flagship employment scheme guarantees at least 100 days of unskilled wage employment in a financial year to every rural household. MGNREGA aims to provide social security, enhance livelihood security, and promote rural infrastructure development.
- **Pradhan Mantri Awas Yojana (PMAY):** Launched to provide affordable housing to the urban poor, PMAY seeks to ensure that every Indian has access to a safe and secure shelter. The scheme emphasizes the construction of houses with basic amenities, thereby improving living conditions for low-income families.
- **Ujjwala Yojana:** This initiative aims to provide clean cooking fuel (LPG) to women from Below Poverty Line (BPL) households, reducing reliance on traditional biomass fuels that pose health risks and contribute to environmental degradation.
- **Jan Dhan Yojana:** This financial inclusion program promotes access to banking services for the unbanked population, aiming to empower individuals by providing them with bank accounts, credit, insurance, and pension schemes.
- **National Food Security Act (NFSA):** Enacted to ensure food security for the vulnerable sections of society, the NFSA provides subsidized food grains to eligible households, aiming to alleviate hunger and malnutrition.

2. Political Motivations Behind Welfare Schemes

Welfare schemes often serve multiple purposes beyond their stated objectives. Politically, they can be leveraged for electoral gains, social stability, and strengthening party loyalty. Here are some key motivations driving the implementation of welfare schemes:

- **Electoral Considerations:** Politicians frequently introduce welfare schemes in response to electoral pressures. By addressing the needs of specific constituencies, political parties aim to secure votes and maintain power. For instance, the introduction of the MGNREGA was viewed as a strategic move to consolidate support in rural areas during elections.
- **Political Branding:** Welfare schemes contribute to a party's brand image by showcasing its commitment to social justice and development. Successful implementation of such programs enhances the reputation of ruling parties, fostering a perception of effective governance.
- **Mobilization of Support:** Political leaders often use welfare schemes as tools to mobilize support from specific demographic groups. By tailoring programs to meet the unique needs of particular communities—such as women, farmers, or minorities—politicians can garner loyalty and reinforce their voter base.
- **Reduction of Social Unrest:** Welfare schemes are also seen as mechanisms to reduce social unrest and promote stability. By addressing the basic needs of citizens, governments can mitigate dissatisfaction and prevent protests or movements that may threaten their authority.

3. Impact on Society

Welfare schemes play a vital role in enhancing the socio-economic conditions of beneficiaries. They contribute to:

- **Poverty Alleviation:** Many welfare programs have been instrumental in lifting families out of poverty, providing them with financial assistance, employment opportunities, and essential services. For instance, MGNREGA has significantly improved rural livelihoods by ensuring a steady income.

- **Empowerment of Women:** Initiatives like Ujjwala Yojana and Jan Dhan Yojana empower women by providing them with access to clean energy and financial resources. By reducing the burden of household chores and enhancing financial independence, these schemes contribute to gender equality.
- **Health and Nutrition:** Programs targeting food security, health care, and sanitation help improve the overall health and nutritional status of vulnerable populations. By ensuring access to adequate food and healthcare services, these schemes reduce malnutrition and promote well-being.
- **Social Inclusion:** Welfare schemes promote social inclusion by addressing the needs of marginalized communities. They provide a safety net for the economically disadvantaged and create pathways for upward mobility.

4. Challenges and Criticisms

Despite the positive impact of welfare schemes, several challenges and criticisms persist:

- **Leakages and Corruption:** A significant concern is the leakage of funds and corruption in the implementation of welfare schemes. Mismanagement and lack of transparency can undermine the effectiveness of these programs, limiting their reach and impact.
- **Dependence on Political Will:** The success of welfare schemes often hinges on the political commitment of ruling parties. Changes in government can lead to discontinuation or alteration of programs, affecting beneficiaries' access to essential services.
- **Targeting and Inclusion Errors:** Many welfare schemes face challenges related to targeting the right beneficiaries. Inaccu-

rate identification of eligible households can result in exclusion errors, leaving deserving individuals without support.
- **Sustainability:** Some welfare schemes may not be sustainable in the long run, particularly if they rely heavily on government funding without a clear strategy for generating revenue or creating self-sustaining mechanisms.

Welfare schemes are a vital component of India's socio-political landscape, reflecting the government's commitment to addressing the needs of its citizens. While they have the potential to drive significant social change and improve quality of life, the interplay of political motivations, implementation challenges, and societal impacts highlights the complexity of welfare politics in India. To maximize their effectiveness, it is crucial for policymakers to ensure transparency, accountability, and sustainability in these programs while remaining responsive to the evolving needs of the population. Ultimately, welfare schemes should serve as instruments of empowerment, fostering a more equitable and inclusive society.

Development Politics: The Interplay of Infrastructure and Political Promises

Development politics in India encapsulates the complex relationship between political decision-making and the execution of infrastructure projects aimed at fostering economic growth and social progress. This interplay often shapes the political landscape, influencing electoral outcomes and shaping public perception of governance. In this section, we will explore how development politics operates in India, focusing on the motivations behind major infrastructure projects, their socio-economic implications, and the political dynamics at play.

1. Infrastructure as a Political Tool

In India, infrastructure development has become a pivotal element of political strategy. Political leaders often view infrastructure projects as vital means to demonstrate effective governance and to fulfill electoral promises. These projects range from roads and railways to power plants and urban development initiatives. The rationale behind this focus on infrastructure includes:

- **Visibility and Tangibility:** Infrastructure projects are highly visible and tangible. They provide immediate evidence of a government's efforts to improve the quality of life for its citizens. A newly constructed highway, for example, can symbolize progress and development, making it a compelling narrative for political leaders.
- **Job Creation:** Large infrastructure projects typically generate substantial employment opportunities, addressing one of the critical issues in Indian politics: unemployment. By promoting job creation, political leaders can directly influence voter sentiments and gain popular support.
- **Economic Growth:** Development projects are often linked to economic growth. Political leaders can leverage the promise of economic development to rally support, emphasizing how infrastructure improvements can attract investment, enhance productivity, and ultimately lead to better living standards.

2. Electoral Promises and Development Schemes

Development politics is characterized by a cycle of electoral promises and project implementation. Politicians often announce ambitious infrastructure projects during election campaigns, pledging to fulfill them if elected. This practice raises several critical considerations:

- **Promise vs. Reality:** The gap between promises made during campaigns and the actual implementation of projects can lead to disillusionment among voters. When elected leaders fail to deliver on their commitments, it can result in a loss of credibility and trust in political institutions.

- **Political Patronage:** The allocation of resources for development projects can sometimes be influenced by political considerations rather than objective needs. Politicians may prioritize projects in constituencies where they seek to consolidate their electoral base, leading to uneven development across regions.
- **Long-Term Planning vs. Short-Term Gains:** Development politics often focuses on short-term gains to win immediate electoral support, potentially at the expense of long-term planning and sustainability. This can result in poorly conceived projects that fail to address the underlying issues faced by communities.

3. Major Infrastructure Projects and Political Dynamics

Several key infrastructure projects have defined the landscape of development politics in India. These projects not only aim to enhance the country's infrastructure but also reflect the political strategies employed by various governments. Here are a few notable examples:

- **Mumbai Coastal Road Project:** This ambitious project aims to improve connectivity along the coast of Mumbai, addressing traffic congestion and promoting economic activity. The project has been met with mixed reactions, reflecting concerns over environmental impact and displacement of local communities. Politically, it serves as a focal point for the ruling party to showcase its commitment to urban development.
- **Bullet Train Project:** The proposed Mumbai-Ahmedabad high-speed rail corridor is a flagship initiative aimed at modernizing India's railway infrastructure. While the project promises faster travel and economic benefits, it has also sparked debates over funding, land acquisition, and potential displacement of communities, highlighting the challenges of balancing development with social considerations.
- **Smart Cities Mission:** Launched in 2015, this initiative aims to create smart urban spaces equipped with sustainable infra-

structure and improved services. The mission aligns with the political narrative of promoting modernization and urbanization, yet it raises questions about the inclusivity and accessibility of urban development.

4. Socio-Economic Implications of Development Politics

The interplay of development politics and infrastructure projects has far-reaching socio-economic implications:

- **Displacement and Land Acquisition:** Many large-scale infrastructure projects involve the acquisition of land, which can lead to displacement of local communities. This raises ethical questions about the rights of affected individuals and the responsibility of governments to address their grievances.
- **Environmental Concerns:** Development projects often have significant environmental impacts, including habitat destruction and pollution. Balancing economic growth with environmental sustainability remains a critical challenge in development politics.
- **Regional Disparities:** Development projects may exacerbate regional disparities if resources are disproportionately allocated to certain areas. Ensuring equitable development across all regions is essential to foster social harmony and national integration.

5. The Role of Civil Society and Grassroots Movements

Civil society and grassroots movements play a crucial role in shaping development politics in India. Activists, NGOs, and community organizations often advocate for the rights of marginalized communities, raising awareness about the social and environmental implications of infrastructure projects. Their involvement can lead to:

- **Accountability and Transparency:** Advocacy groups often demand greater accountability from governments regarding the implementation of development projects, pushing for transparency in decision-making processes.

- **Participatory Governance:** Grassroots movements can promote participatory governance by involving local communities in the planning and execution of development projects. This ensures that projects are aligned with the needs and aspirations of the people they affect.

6. Challenges and the Road Ahead

Despite the potential of development politics to drive positive change, several challenges persist:

- **Corruption and Mismanagement:** Corruption in the allocation and execution of development projects can undermine their effectiveness and erode public trust in government institutions.
- **Political Rivalries:** Political rivalries can hinder collaborative efforts to implement development projects, resulting in stalled initiatives and wasted resources.
- **Need for Comprehensive Planning:** A lack of comprehensive planning that integrates social, economic, and environmental considerations can lead to unsustainable development outcomes.

Development politics in India embodies the intricate relationship between political decision-making and infrastructure development. As governments strive to fulfill their electoral promises through major projects, the implications of these initiatives extend beyond mere economic growth. The interplay of political motivations, societal needs, and grassroots activism shapes the trajectory of development, highlighting the necessity for accountable and inclusive governance. Moving forward, a focus on sustainable practices, community involvement, and equitable resource allocation will be essential to harness the full potential of development politics, ensuring that the benefits of progress are shared by all segments of society.

Case Studies and Analysis: Understanding Development Politics Through Real-World Examples

To grasp the nuances of development politics in India, it is essential to analyze specific case studies that highlight the interplay between political decisions and infrastructure projects. These examples illustrate how political promises shape development initiatives and how the outcomes of these projects impact society, economics, and governance. Below, we delve into a few significant case studies that provide insight into the challenges and successes of development politics in India.

1. The Delhi-Mumbai Industrial Corridor (DMIC)

Overview: The DMIC is one of India's most ambitious infrastructure projects, aimed at creating a high-tech industrial zone between Delhi and Mumbai. This 1,500 km-long corridor is expected to significantly enhance the economic landscape of the regions it traverses.

Political Context: Launched in 2006, the DMIC project has seen successive governments champion its importance for boosting industrial growth and employment. The project received strong backing from the central government, which viewed it as a means to improve India's global competitiveness.

Key Outcomes:

- **Economic Growth:** The DMIC is expected to generate over 1 million jobs and attract significant foreign investment, thus stimulating economic growth in the region.
- **Regional Development:** Several new industrial towns and smart cities are being planned along the corridor, aiming to redistribute economic activity and reduce regional disparities.
- **Challenges:** Despite its potential, the DMIC has faced delays due to land acquisition issues, bureaucratic hurdles, and en-

vironmental concerns. Local resistance and inadequate infrastructure in peripheral areas remain significant challenges to successful implementation.

Analysis: The DMIC illustrates how development politics can mobilize resources for significant infrastructure projects while also highlighting the need for efficient governance and stakeholder engagement. The project's success hinges on balancing economic aspirations with the social and environmental needs of affected communities.

2. Narmada Valley Project (Sardar Sarovar Dam)

Overview: The Sardar Sarovar Dam, part of the Narmada Valley Development Project, was constructed to provide irrigation, hydroelectric power, and drinking water to millions across Gujarat, Maharashtra, and Madhya Pradesh.

Political Context: Initiated in the 1960s and completed in 2017, the dam project has been a focal point of political debates regarding development, displacement, and environmental sustainability. It attracted both strong governmental support and significant opposition from various activist groups.

Key Outcomes:

- **Economic Impact:** The dam has helped in irrigation expansion and electricity generation, contributing to agricultural productivity and energy needs in the region.
- **Displacement Issues:** The project displaced thousands of families, leading to protests and activism led by groups like the Narmada Bachao Andolan (NBA), which advocated for the rights of displaced persons and demanded fair compensation and rehabilitation.
- **Environmental Concerns:** The dam's construction raised serious environmental issues, including changes to local ecosystems and potential adverse impacts on biodiversity.

Analysis: The Narmada Valley Project serves as a case study of the conflict between large-scale development and social justice. It emphasizes the need for inclusive planning that considers the voices of marginalized communities and environmental sustainability in the pursuit of economic growth.

3. Pradhan Mantri Awas Yojana (PMAY)

Overview: Launched in 2015, the PMAY aims to provide affordable housing to the urban poor by 2022. The scheme seeks to build over 20 million affordable homes across the country.

Political Context: The PMAY has been a flagship initiative of the current government, emphasizing its commitment to "Housing for All." The program's success is viewed as critical to gaining political favor among lower-income voters, especially in urban areas.

Key Outcomes:

- **Housing Accessibility:** The initiative has facilitated home-ownership among the economically weaker sections, significantly improving living conditions.
- **Economic Stimulus:** The construction activity associated with the PMAY has generated jobs in the construction sector, stimulating economic growth.
- **Implementation Challenges:** Despite its objectives, the program has faced challenges related to bureaucratic inefficiencies, quality control in construction, and disparities in implementation across states.

Analysis: The PMAY demonstrates how development politics can focus on social welfare while simultaneously addressing housing shortages. However, the effectiveness of such schemes often hinges on transparent implementation, accountability, and active community participation.

4. The National Highways Development Project (NHDP)

Overview: The NHDP, initiated in the late 1990s, is a significant infrastructure program aimed at upgrading and expanding India's national highways to enhance connectivity and promote economic development.

Political Context: The project has received bipartisan support as improving road infrastructure is seen as essential for economic growth and development. Various governments have emphasized the importance of this initiative to improve trade and transport efficiency.

Key Outcomes:

- **Infrastructure Development:** The NHDP has led to the construction of thousands of kilometers of national highways, improving connectivity between major cities and rural areas.
- **Economic Growth:** Improved road infrastructure has facilitated trade, reduced transportation costs, and contributed to economic growth, especially in rural and semi-urban areas.
- **Corruption and Accountability Issues:** The NHDP has also faced challenges, including allegations of corruption in project bidding and execution, highlighting the need for rigorous oversight and accountability.

Analysis: The NHDP exemplifies the potential of development politics to foster economic growth through infrastructure. However, it also underscores the risks of corruption and mismanagement, necessitating robust governance frameworks to ensure successful implementation.

5. Swachh Bharat Abhiyan (Clean India Mission)

Overview: Launched in 2014, Swachh Bharat Abhiyan aims to improve sanitation and cleanliness across India, with a particular focus on eliminating open defecation.

Political Context: The mission was a key initiative of the ruling government and has been used as a political tool to demonstrate commitment to public health and hygiene. It seeks to build a clean India by encouraging citizen participation and government accountability.

Key Outcomes:

- **Increased Sanitation Coverage:** The campaign has significantly increased the number of toilets constructed in rural and urban areas, promoting hygiene and health.
- **Public Awareness:** Swachh Bharat Abhiyan has raised awareness about sanitation issues, encouraging community involvement and behavior change.
- **Implementation Challenges:** Despite its successes, challenges remain in terms of ensuring the sustainability of infrastructure and continuous community engagement.

Analysis: Swachh Bharat Abhiyan highlights how development politics can be effectively aligned with social welfare objectives. It demonstrates the power of public campaigns in changing social norms, while also emphasizing the importance of sustainable practices to maintain progress.

The case studies analyzed above illustrate the complexities and dynamics of development politics in India. They reveal how political motivations, public needs, and socio-economic factors intertwine in shaping infrastructure initiatives. As India continues to navigate its path towards progress, understanding these dynamics becomes crucial for ensuring that development serves as a tool for inclusive growth and social justice. The lessons learned from these case studies can inform future policy decisions and the implementation of infrastructure projects, emphasizing the importance of stakeholder engagement, transparency, and sustainable practices.

Conclusion: The Politics of Welfare and Development

The interplay between politics and development in India is complex and multifaceted, as evidenced by the diverse welfare schemes and development projects initiated over the years. As we have explored throughout this chapter, the success and efficacy of these initiatives often hinge on the political will, the strategic vision of leaders, and the participation of the citizenry.

Reflecting on Welfare Schemes

Welfare schemes such as Mahatma Gandhi National Rural Employment Guarantee Act (MGNREGA), Ujjwala Yojana, and Jan Dhan Yojana have showcased the government's commitment to improving the living standards of marginalized communities. These programs not only aim to address immediate needs but also seek to empower citizens through skill development, financial inclusion, and access to essential services. However, the effectiveness of these schemes varies significantly based on local governance, implementation challenges, and the extent of public engagement.

The Role of Development Politics

Development politics plays a pivotal role in shaping the trajectory of infrastructure projects, such as the Mumbai Coastal Road and the Mumbai-Ahmedabad Bullet Train. These initiatives highlight the balancing act between economic growth, political promises, and public sentiment. While they have the potential to transform urban landscapes and enhance connectivity, they also evoke concerns about displacement, environmental impact, and equitable resource distribution. Political accountability and transparent decision-making are crucial in mitigating these challenges and ensuring that development benefits all sections of society.

Analyzing the Future of Welfare and Development

As India moves forward, the challenge lies in fostering a development model that is inclusive and sustainable. This requires a shift from mere political rhetoric to genuine action, focusing on collaboration between the government, civil society, and local communities. The role of civil society in holding governments accountable, advocating for rights, and ensuring the equitable distribution of resources is indispensable.

Moreover, as the nation faces emerging issues such as climate change, urbanization, and technological advancement, it is imperative for welfare policies to adapt and evolve. Future initiatives must be rooted in a long-term vision that prioritizes sustainability, resilience, and social justice, ensuring that the benefits of development reach the most vulnerable populations.

Call to Action

In conclusion, the politics of welfare and development in India represents a critical nexus of power, policy, and citizen engagement. It calls for an informed and active citizenry that holds political leaders accountable and advocates for a more equitable society. As young people and future leaders, it is essential to remain engaged in the political process, ensuring that welfare and development initiatives not only serve immediate needs but also lay the groundwork for a just and prosperous future for all.

As we continue to reflect on the successes and challenges of welfare schemes and development projects, let us commit to fostering a political culture that prioritizes transparency, accountability, and inclusivity, paving the way for a brighter future for India. By learning from past experiences and actively participating in shaping policies, we can collectively work towards a nation where welfare and development are accessible to every citizen, driving meaningful change and progress.

PART V: CHANGING THE FUTURE

| 14 |

Role of Youth in Politics

The active involvement of youth in politics is crucial for shaping the future of India's democracy and governance. This chapter explores the significance of youth participation, their impact through movements and activism, and avenues for young individuals to engage in political processes effectively.

Why Young People Matter

In the contemporary political landscape, the role of young people is more crucial than ever. As the demographic backbone of the nation, youth not only represent a significant portion of the population but also possess the potential to drive transformative change in society. Here are several reasons why young people matter in politics:

1. Demographic Dividend

India, with over 600 million individuals under the age of 25, stands at the forefront of a demographic revolution. This youthful population presents a unique opportunity for the country, as they are poised to become the engine of economic growth and social change. Young people bring fresh perspectives, energy, and enthusiasm, which are essential for invigorating the political process and addressing the challenges of today.

2. Voter Turnout and Engagement

Young voters have historically demonstrated lower turnout rates compared to older demographics. However, this trend is shifting. With increasing awareness of their rights and the impact of political decisions on their futures, young people are becoming more engaged in the electoral process. Their participation in elections not only shapes political outcomes but also encourages political parties to address issues pertinent to their interests, such as education, employment, and climate change.

3. Advocacy for Change

Young people are often at the forefront of social movements and advocacy campaigns. They are unafraid to challenge the status quo and demand accountability from their leaders. Movements such as the protests against the Citizenship Amendment Act (CAA) and environmental activism led by youth highlight their capacity to mobilize, organize, and influence public opinion. By leveraging social media and technology, young activists can amplify their voices and reach a broader audience, fostering a culture of activism and engagement.

4. Innovative Ideas and Solutions

Youth are often more attuned to global trends, technological advancements, and emerging challenges. Their familiarity with digital tools and platforms equips them to think creatively and propose innovative solutions to complex issues. This potential for fresh ideas is critical in an era where traditional political strategies may not be sufficient to address new challenges, such as climate change, economic disparity, and social justice.

5. Breaking Down Barriers

Young people can challenge entrenched norms and societal expectations, promoting inclusivity and diversity in politics. They often advocate for equal representation across gender, caste, and socioeconomic lines, pushing for policies that address systemic inequalities. Their willingness to engage in dialogue and collaborate across different groups fosters a more inclusive political environment, where multiple voices can be heard and considered.

6. Future Leaders and Decision-Makers

Investing in youth leadership is essential for the long-term health of democracy. By engaging young people in political processes, mentoring them, and providing opportunities for leadership roles, society can cultivate the next generation of decision-makers. This engagement ensures that the interests and perspectives of youth are reflected in governance, creating policies that are responsive to their needs.

7. Civic Responsibility and Awareness

Young people have a unique capacity to promote civic responsibility among their peers. Their involvement in politics encourages discussions around rights, responsibilities, and the importance of active citizenship. Through educational initiatives and community engagement, they can help foster a politically aware society that values democratic principles and processes.

In summary, young people matter in politics for their ability to catalyze change, engage in the electoral process, and advocate for inclusive policies. Their energy, creativity, and commitment to social justice can reshape the political landscape and pave the way for a more equitable future. By empowering youth and recognizing their contributions, society can harness their potential to create meaningful change, ensuring that the voices of the next generation are not only heard but also prioritized in the political arena.

Youth Movements and Activism

Youth movements and activism play a pivotal role in shaping the political landscape, influencing policies, and advocating for social justice. Throughout history, young people have mobilized to challenge injustices, raise awareness about pressing issues, and demand change. In India, this trend has gained significant momentum in recent years, driven by a combination of socio-economic factors, technological advancements, and a growing sense of civic responsibility among the youth. Here's an expanded look at the various facets of youth movements and activism in India:

1. Historical Context of Youth Activism

The roots of youth activism in India can be traced back to the freedom struggle, where young leaders like Bhagat Singh and Subhas Chandra Bose emerged as influential figures. Their passion, courage, and commitment to independence inspired a generation to fight against colonial rule. This historical legacy continues to resonate today, instilling a sense of purpose among young people who seek to effect change in their communities.

2. Emergence of Contemporary Movements

In recent years, several youth-led movements have gained national attention, demonstrating the power of collective action. These movements often arise in response to specific issues, reflecting the concerns and aspirations of the younger generation. Some notable examples include:

- **CAA Protests**: The protests against the Citizenship Amendment Act (CAA) saw young people mobilizing across the country, particularly in universities. They raised questions about secularism, discrimination, and national identity, challenging the government's narrative and advocating for inclusivity.
- **Environmental Activism**: Inspired by global movements, Indian youth have taken to the streets to demand action on climate change. Initiatives like Fridays for Future, inspired by Greta Thunberg, have encouraged young activists to organize rallies, workshops, and campaigns, urging the government to prioritize environmental sustainability.
- **Anti-Rape Protests**: In the aftermath of high-profile cases of sexual violence, youth-led protests have emerged, calling for justice and systemic changes in law enforcement and social attitudes towards women. These movements highlight the urgent need for gender equality and the protection of women's rights.

3. Role of Technology and Social Media

The advent of technology and social media has revolutionized youth activism. Platforms like Twitter, Facebook, and Instagram enable young activists to communicate, organize, and amplify their messages quickly. Social media serves as a powerful tool for:

- **Raising Awareness**: Youth can share information about social issues, mobilize support, and educate their peers about critical topics. Hashtags and viral campaigns often bring attention to causes that may otherwise go unnoticed.
- **Building Networks**: Online platforms facilitate the formation of networks among activists, allowing them to collaborate across geographic boundaries. This interconnectedness fosters solidarity and strengthens the impact of movements.
- **Real-Time Mobilization**: Social media allows for quick mobilization of supporters, enabling young people to organize protests and events at a moment's notice. This agility is crucial in responding to emerging issues and holding authorities accountable.

4. Collaborations with Civil Society

Many youth movements have collaborated with civil society organizations, NGOs, and other advocacy groups to amplify their impact. These partnerships provide essential resources, expertise, and support in organizing campaigns and lobbying for policy changes. For example, during the CAA protests, student unions collaborated with various human rights organizations to articulate their demands and ensure their voices were heard at national forums.

5. Challenges Faced by Youth Activists

Despite their potential, youth activists often encounter several challenges:

- **Repression and Intimidation**: Many young activists face harassment, intimidation, or even legal action for expressing dissent. Government crackdowns on protests can discourage participation and create an atmosphere of fear.

- **Fragmentation**: The diversity of issues and causes can lead to fragmentation within youth movements. While this diversity is valuable, it can also dilute focus and make it difficult to present a united front.
- **Limited Political Representation**: Youth often find it challenging to influence formal political structures. Many political parties do not prioritize the issues that matter to young people, leading to a disconnect between activists and decision-makers.

6. The Future of Youth Activism in India

As India moves forward, the role of youth in politics and activism is expected to grow. With increasing awareness of their rights and the potential for change, young people are likely to continue mobilizing around issues such as climate change, gender equality, education, and economic justice. Their ability to harness technology and connect with global movements positions them as key players in shaping the future of Indian democracy.

In conclusion, youth movements and activism are essential components of a vibrant democracy. They serve as a catalyst for social change, giving voice to the concerns of young people and challenging the status quo. By actively participating in the political process, advocating for their rights, and mobilizing for justice, young people in India can drive transformative change and pave the way for a more inclusive and equitable society. The energy and passion of youth hold the promise of a brighter future, where their voices are heard and valued in shaping the nation's trajectory.

Running for Office

Running for political office is a powerful way for young people to effect change and influence policy. It offers an opportunity to bring fresh perspectives and ideas into the political arena, ensuring that the voices of the younger generation are represented in decision-making processes. However, entering the political landscape can be challenging, especially for first-time candidates. Here, we will explore the essential steps and considerations for young people aspiring to run for office in India, the importance of representation, and the potential impact they can have.

1. Understanding the Political Landscape

Before launching a campaign, it is crucial to understand the political landscape in which one is operating. This includes:

- **Political Structure**: Familiarize yourself with the political system, including the roles and responsibilities of various offices, such as local councils, state assemblies, and the Parliament. Understanding how these bodies function and the issues they address will inform your campaign strategy.
- **Current Issues**: Stay informed about the pressing issues in your community and the nation. This could range from education and employment to environmental sustainability and social justice. Understanding these issues will help you connect with voters and develop relevant policies.
- **Political Parties**: Consider the political party you want to align with or whether to run as an independent candidate. Research the ideologies and values of different parties and identify which aligns with your vision and goals. Joining a party can provide support and resources, while running independently may allow for more flexibility in addressing local issues.

2. Building a Support Network

A successful campaign relies on a strong support network. Here are key components to consider:

- **Mentorship**: Seek out mentors who have experience in politics or community organizing. They can offer guidance, share insights, and help navigate challenges you may face as a candidate.
- **Volunteers**: Assemble a team of dedicated volunteers who share your vision and can assist with campaign activities. Mo-

bilizing a group of passionate supporters can help amplify your message and extend your reach within the community.

- **Community Engagement**: Engage with your community to build relationships and trust. Attend local events, hold town hall meetings, and listen to the concerns of constituents. Building a strong rapport with the community will enhance your credibility and encourage voter support.

3. Developing a Campaign Strategy

A clear campaign strategy is essential for reaching voters and communicating your vision effectively. Key elements include:

- **Messaging**: Craft a compelling message that resonates with voters. Clearly articulate your goals, values, and the changes you wish to implement. Personal stories and experiences can enhance relatability and inspire voters.
- **Target Audience**: Identify your target demographic and tailor your campaign efforts accordingly. Understanding the needs and concerns of different groups—such as students, professionals, or marginalized communities—will help you address their specific issues and garner support.
- **Campaign Plan**: Develop a comprehensive campaign plan outlining your objectives, timeline, budget, and tactics. Include methods for reaching voters, such as door-to-door canvassing, social media outreach, and public speaking engagements.

4. Navigating the Electoral Process

Understanding the electoral process is critical for any candidate. Key steps include:

- **Filing Nominations**: Familiarize yourself with the legal requirements for candidacy, including filing nominations and submitting necessary documentation. Each office has specific criteria, such as age, residency, and financial disclosures.

- **Election Commission Guidelines**: Adhere to the guidelines set forth by the Election Commission of India, which governs the conduct of elections. This includes rules on campaign financing, advertising, and ethical campaigning.
- **Voter Engagement**: Encourage voter registration and turnout. Engage with constituents to educate them about the voting process and the importance of participating in elections. Create initiatives to mobilize young voters and ensure their voices are heard at the ballot box.

5. Facing Challenges and Overcoming Barriers

Running for office can be fraught with challenges, particularly for young candidates:

- **Financial Constraints**: Campaigning can be expensive, and many young candidates may struggle to secure funding. Explore options for campaign financing, such as small donations from supporters, crowdfunding, or party assistance.
- **Public Scrutiny**: As a candidate, you will be under public scrutiny. Prepare to handle criticism, negative campaigning, and media coverage. Maintaining transparency and integrity will help build trust with voters.
- **Balancing Responsibilities**: Managing a campaign while juggling education, work, or other commitments can be demanding. Time management and prioritization are essential skills to develop to ensure you can dedicate the necessary time to your campaign.

6. The Importance of Representation

Having young people in political office is crucial for a well-rounded and inclusive democracy. Young leaders can:

- **Challenge Established Norms**: They bring fresh ideas and perspectives, challenging the status quo and encouraging innovation in policy-making.
- **Address Youth Concerns**: Young elected officials are better equipped to understand and address the specific issues that affect their peers, such as education, employment, and mental health.
- **Inspire Civic Engagement**: By running for office, young leaders can inspire their peers to engage in politics and contribute to the democratic process. Their involvement can mobilize a generation to become more politically active and invested in their communities.

A Call to Action

Running for political office is a courageous and impactful way for young people to make a difference in their communities and shape the future of India. With determination, a clear vision, and a commitment to serving the public, young candidates can challenge established norms, advocate for change, and inspire others to follow in their footsteps. By taking the leap into politics, they can ensure that the voices of the youth are represented and that the nation's future is shaped by the ideals and aspirations of its younger generation.

Case Studies and Inspirations

The journey of young politicians in India is marked by significant achievements, innovative approaches, and transformative movements. By examining case studies of young leaders and grassroots movements, we can draw inspiration and lessons for aspiring candidates. Here, we highlight some noteworthy examples that demonstrate the potential for youth to influence political change in India.

1. Kanhaiya Kumar: A Voice of Resistance

Kanhaiya Kumar, former president of the Jawaharlal Nehru University Students' Union (JNUSU), gained national prominence for his articulate speeches and activism against various government policies. In 2016, he was arrested on charges of sedition after a controversial event at JNU, which sparked widespread protests across the country. Kanhaiya emerged as a symbol of youth resistance against authoritarianism, advocating for free speech, social justice, and inclusive politics.

Lessons Learned:

- **Courage in the Face of Adversity**: Kanhaiya's ability to stand firm against governmental pressure highlighted the importance of resilience and courage in political activism.
- **Utilizing Platforms**: His experience underscores the power of educational institutions as platforms for political engagement and mobilization.
- **Articulation of Ideas**: Kanhaiya's eloquent communication style resonated with youth, demonstrating the significance of effective messaging in reaching and engaging constituents.

2. Tushar Singh: Engaging Youth Through Social Media

Tushar Singh, a young leader from Uttar Pradesh, leveraged social media to mobilize youth for political change. He founded an online campaign called "Youth for Change," which aimed to raise awareness about local governance issues, such as education, employment, and public health. By utilizing platforms like Instagram, Twitter, and Facebook, Tushar was able to engage thousands of young voters, encouraging them to participate in the electoral process.

Lessons Learned:

- **Digital Engagement**: Tushar's case illustrates the effectiveness of digital tools in reaching a broader audience and fostering political engagement among youth.
- **Community-Centric Approach**: His focus on local issues resonated with constituents, emphasizing the importance of addressing specific community needs in political campaigns.

- **Building Networks**: Tushar successfully created a network of young activists, highlighting the power of collaboration and collective action in driving change.

3. Vivek Sunder: Youth in Local Governance

Vivek Sunder, a 27-year-old elected representative in his local panchayat in Tamil Nadu, embodies the potential for youth to influence local governance. His campaign focused on issues like waste management, water conservation, and women's empowerment. By actively engaging with his constituents and prioritizing their concerns, Vivek successfully implemented several initiatives, enhancing community participation and fostering a sense of ownership among residents.

Lessons Learned:

- **Grassroots Focus**: Vivek's success underscores the significance of local governance in effecting change and improving community well-being.
- **Engagement with Constituents**: Regular interaction with the community fosters trust and transparency, essential for effective representation.
- **Practical Solutions**: His focus on actionable policies demonstrates that young leaders can address pressing issues and create tangible impacts in their communities.

4. Swaathi Rao: Environmental Activism and Politics

Swaathi Rao, a young environmental activist from Maharashtra, has been instrumental in advocating for sustainable policies and climate action. Her grassroots organization, "Green India Youth," mobilizes young people to participate in environmental conservation efforts and engage with local authorities on sustainability initiatives. Swaathi's activism has led to the implementation of eco-friendly practices in her community and inspired many youth to join the cause.

Lessons Learned:

- **Passion for Causes**: Swaathi's dedication to environmental issues exemplifies how personal passion can translate into political action.
- **Mobilizing Youth for Change**: Her ability to inspire and organize youth around a common cause highlights the potential for grassroots movements to shape policy.
- **Intersectionality in Politics**: Swaathi's work illustrates the importance of addressing interconnected issues, such as environmental sustainability and social justice, in political discourse.

5. Youth-Led Movements: The CAA Protests

The Citizenship Amendment Act (CAA) protests in India showcased the power of youth activism in the political landscape. Across the country, young people organized demonstrations, rallies, and sit-ins to voice their dissent against the perceived discriminatory nature of the legislation. The protests were marked by a spirit of unity and resilience, with youth from diverse backgrounds coming together to defend their rights and uphold the values of democracy.

Lessons Learned:

- **Collective Action**: The CAA protests highlighted the strength of collective action in advocating for social justice and human rights.
- **Diverse Voices**: The movement included voices from various communities, demonstrating the importance of inclusivity and intersectionality in political movements.
- **Use of Art and Culture**: Protesters used art, music, and poetry to convey their messages, showcasing the creative ways youth can engage in political discourse.

These case studies illustrate the diverse paths young leaders can take to enter politics and advocate for change. Through their passion, resilience, and innovative approaches, these individuals have inspired many others to engage in the political process and work toward a better future. By learning from these examples, aspiring young politicians can find motivation and guidance in their own journeys to effect change in their communities and beyond.

Conclusion

The role of youth in politics is not just a peripheral aspect of the political landscape; it is integral to the functioning of a vibrant democracy. As we've explored throughout this chapter, young people are uniquely positioned to influence the political discourse in India, leveraging their energy, creativity, and passion for social justice to advocate for change.

The empowerment of youth is critical for several reasons. First, young individuals bring fresh perspectives that can challenge outdated norms and practices. Their engagement in political processes ensures that issues pertinent to their generation, such as climate change, employment, education, and social equity, are brought to the forefront of policy discussions. Moreover, the ability of youth to harness technology and social media has transformed the way political campaigns are conducted and issues are discussed. This shift has opened new avenues for engagement, making it easier for young people to mobilize, inform, and influence their peers and communities.

However, the journey is not without challenges. The prevailing political environment can often seem unwelcoming to newcomers, and systemic barriers such as entrenched party structures, societal norms, and, at times, the lack of resources can deter youth from participating. It is crucial for young leaders to navigate these obstacles while remaining resilient and committed to their causes. The examples of successful youth movements and leaders presented earlier serve as beacons of hope and sources of inspiration, showing that change is indeed possible.

In addition to advocating for their rights and interests, young people must also recognize their responsibilities as citizens. Active participation in the electoral process—whether through voting, campaigning, or running for office—is vital for ensuring that their voices are heard and represented. Furthermore, fostering dialogue across generational divides can help build a more inclusive political culture where the ideas and concerns of all citizens are valued.

As we look toward the future, it is evident that the political landscape in India will be significantly shaped by the engagement of its youth. By harnessing their collective power, young people have the potential to redefine what is possible in politics, championing causes that reflect their values and aspirations. It is a call to action for the younger generation: to be informed, engaged, and proactive participants in shaping the future of their country.

In conclusion, the role of youth in politics is not merely about their presence but about the transformative impact they can have on the political arena. As they continue to mobilize, advocate, and innovate, the potential for meaningful change becomes limitless. By seizing the moment and stepping into leadership roles, young people can contribute to a more just, equitable, and democratic society.

| 15 |

The Future of Indian Politics

The landscape of Indian politics is evolving rapidly, shaped by the forces of digital technology, emerging electoral reforms, and a shifting global context. This chapter explores how these factors are reshaping the political arena, with a focus on digital politics, potential reforms, and India's role on the global stage.

Digital Politics: The New Frontier of Political Engagement

In the 21st century, digital technology has dramatically reshaped every aspect of society, including politics. In India, where a significant portion of the population is young and tech-savvy, the rise of digital politics marks a pivotal shift in how political engagement occurs. This transformation is driven by the pervasive use of social media, online platforms, and digital communication, fundamentally altering political campaigns, public discourse, and civic participation.

The Role of Social Media

Social media platforms like Facebook, Twitter, Instagram, and WhatsApp have become vital tools for political communication and engagement. Political parties and candidates use these platforms to reach voters directly, bypassing traditional media channels. This direct communication allows for a more personalized approach, enabling politicians to engage with their constituents on a more intimate level. They can share their policies, respond to questions, and gather feedback in real time.

The influence of social media extends beyond communication. It serves as a powerful mobilization tool for grassroots movements. Campaigns can be organized and amplified quickly, reaching vast audiences within minutes. For instance, movements such as #MeToo and climate strikes have gained traction largely through social media, showcasing how digital platforms can galvanize public opinion and drive social change.

Data Analytics and Targeted Campaigns

In addition to social media, the use of data analytics has revolutionized political campaigns. Political parties now collect and analyze vast amounts of data to understand voter behavior, preferences, and demographics. This data-driven approach allows for targeted campaigning, where messages are tailored to specific audiences based on their interests and concerns.

For example, during elections, parties utilize algorithms to determine which voters to target with particular advertisements or messages, optimizing their outreach efforts. This precision can lead to more effective campaigns, but it also raises ethical questions about privacy, consent, and the manipulation of public opinion.

Online Activism and E-Governance

The rise of digital politics also facilitates online activism, allowing citizens to organize and advocate for issues they care about without the need for traditional hierarchical structures. Online petitions, campaigns, and movements can gain momentum quickly, often leading to tangible political responses. Activism has evolved to encompass not only protests and demonstrations but also digital campaigns that seek to influence policy and societal norms.

Moreover, e-governance initiatives have made political processes more transparent and accessible. Citizens can now access government services online, file grievances, and participate in consultations, reducing barriers to engagement. Initiatives like the Digital India campaign aim to enhance the digital infrastructure, promoting transparency, efficiency, and accessibility in governance.

Challenges and Concerns

Despite the many benefits of digital politics, there are also significant challenges and concerns. The spread of misinformation and fake news poses a serious threat to informed political discourse. Social media platforms can amplify false narratives and create echo chambers, where individuals only engage with like-minded perspectives. This polarization can exacerbate societal divides and complicate the political landscape.

Additionally, the digital divide remains a critical issue in India. While urban areas may have widespread internet access, many rural regions still lack reliable connectivity. This disparity can disenfranchise significant segments of the population, hindering their participation in the political process.

The Future of Digital Politics

As India continues to embrace digital technology, the landscape of politics will likely evolve further. Innovations such as blockchain for secure voting, artificial intelligence for better engagement, and augmented reality for immersive campaign experiences could redefine how politics is conducted and experienced.

The future of Indian politics is intertwined with the digital realm. Political engagement is becoming increasingly democratized, allowing more voices to be heard and more citizens to participate in shaping their governance. However, it is essential to address the challenges that accompany this transformation to ensure a healthy and inclusive political environment.

In conclusion, digital politics represents a new frontier for democracy in India. It holds the promise of greater engagement, transparency, and accountability while also posing challenges that require vigilant attention. As political landscapes continue to evolve in the digital age, the capacity of citizens, especially the youth, to harness these tools will play a critical role in shaping the future of Indian democracy.

Future Reforms: Shaping the Political Landscape of India

As India stands on the threshold of a new era, the need for reforms in the political system has never been more pressing. The changing dynamics of society, technology, and global politics demand that the Indian political framework evolves to address contemporary challenges. Future reforms should aim to enhance the democratic process, increase transparency, and foster greater citizen participation. Here are some key areas where reforms could reshape the political landscape in India.

1. Electoral Reforms

Simultaneous Elections: One of the most discussed electoral reforms is the concept of holding simultaneous elections for the Lok Sabha (House of the People) and state legislative assemblies. This approach could reduce the frequency of elections, save costs, and allow the government to focus more on governance rather than perpetual campaigning. It could also minimize the disruptive impact of continuous electoral cycles on development and governance.

Transparency in Party Funding: The issue of political funding has long plagued Indian politics. Reforms aimed at increasing transparency in political donations and expenditures are crucial. Implementing strict regulations on the sources of funding, mandating the disclosure of donations above a certain threshold, and establishing a public funding mechanism for elections can help reduce the influence of money in politics. Transparency can enhance public trust in political parties and reduce corruption.

E-Voting: Introducing e-voting systems can streamline the voting process and increase voter turnout, especially among the youth and tech-savvy population. Secure and user-friendly online voting platforms could make it easier for citizens to exercise their democratic rights. However, this reform must be accompanied by robust cybersecurity measures to protect the integrity of the electoral process.

2. Strengthening Democratic Institutions

Empowering the Election Commission: The Election Commission of India (ECI) plays a critical role in ensuring free and fair elections. Future reforms should focus on empowering the ECI to take stricter actions against electoral malpractices, enhance its autonomy, and provide it with adequate resources to carry out its functions effectively. Strengthening this institution can lead to greater accountability in the electoral process.

Judicial Reforms: The judiciary plays a pivotal role in upholding democracy and protecting citizens' rights. Reforms aimed at expediting the judicial process, increasing the number of judges, and enhancing the efficiency of courts can improve access to justice. Additionally, ensuring the independence of the judiciary from political influence is essential for maintaining the rule of law and safeguarding democratic principles.

3. Enhancing Civic Participation

Promoting Political Education: A well-informed electorate is crucial for a functioning democracy. Future reforms should include initiatives aimed at enhancing political education among citizens, particularly the youth. Educational institutions can incorporate civic education programs that teach students about the political system, rights and responsibilities, and the importance of active participation in democracy.

Encouraging Grassroots Movements: Supporting grassroots movements and local governance can empower communities and encourage greater civic engagement. Reforms that promote decentralization and strengthen local self-governance institutions can provide citizens with a platform to influence decision-making processes directly. This can foster a sense of ownership and responsibility among citizens regarding their governance.

4. Addressing Social Inequalities

Reservation Policies and Social Justice: Future reforms should also focus on addressing social inequalities in representation. While reservation policies for Scheduled Castes, Scheduled Tribes, and Other Backward Classes are essential for ensuring social justice, there is a need to review and possibly expand these policies to include economically weaker sections across all communities. Ensuring diverse representation in political offices can lead to more inclusive governance.

Promoting Gender Equality in Politics: Increasing the participation of women in politics is vital for a balanced and representative democracy. Future reforms could include measures such as reserving seats for women in legislative bodies and encouraging political parties to nominate more women candidates. Empowering women in political spaces can lead to more comprehensive policy-making that considers the diverse needs of society.

5. Leveraging Technology for Governance

Digital Governance: As technology continues to evolve, reforms should leverage digital tools to enhance governance. Initiatives such as online platforms for citizen engagement, e-governance services, and data-driven decision-making can improve the efficiency and transparency of government operations. Using technology to foster communication between citizens and the government can bridge the gap and make governance more responsive.

Artificial Intelligence in Public Policy: Exploring the use of artificial intelligence (AI) and data analytics in public policy can lead to more informed decision-making. By analyzing vast amounts of data, policymakers can gain insights into citizen needs, preferences, and potential policy impacts, leading to more effective and targeted governance strategies.

The future of Indian politics hinges on the ability to adapt and reform in response to changing societal dynamics and technological advancements. By focusing on electoral reforms, strengthening democratic institutions, enhancing civic participation, addressing social inequalities, and leveraging technology for governance, India can pave the way for a more robust and inclusive political landscape.

These reforms are not merely aspirational; they are essential for ensuring that the democratic fabric of India remains resilient in the face of challenges and that every citizen has a voice in shaping the nation's future. The journey ahead requires collective effort, commitment, and a vision for a more equitable and participatory democracy, and it is the responsibility of every stakeholder—citizens, political leaders, and civil society—to work towards this vision.

The Global Stage: India's Political Influence in a Changing World

As India steps confidently into the 21st century, it finds itself at a crucial juncture on the global stage. The nation's political dynamics, economic policies, and strategic decisions not only shape its own destiny but also significantly influence international relations, trade, and global governance. Understanding how Indian politics will affect its global standing over the next decade requires a multifaceted analysis of current trends and potential future developments.

1. Economic Growth and Global Integration

India's impressive economic growth has positioned it as one of the world's largest economies, with the potential to become a global leader in the coming years. The government's focus on initiatives like "Make in India," "Digital India," and "Atmanirbhar Bharat" (Self-Reliant India) aims to enhance manufacturing, foster innovation, and increase self-sufficiency. These economic policies not only promote domestic growth but also attract foreign direct investment (FDI), thereby enhancing India's role in global supply chains.

As India continues to liberalize its economy, it will be better equipped to engage with other nations economically. The growth of a robust middle class in India has expanded consumer markets, making it an attractive destination for international businesses. Additionally, India's engagement in regional trade agreements, such as the Regional Comprehensive Economic Partnership (RCEP), positions it strategically in the Asia-Pacific region, promoting trade and investment ties with neighboring countries.

2. Climate Change and Environmental Leadership

India's political landscape is increasingly shaped by the pressing challenges of climate change and environmental sustainability. As one of the largest carbon emitters, India plays a critical role in global climate negotiations and initiatives. The government's commitment to renewable energy, as highlighted by ambitious targets for solar and wind energy, signals India's readiness to lead in the transition to a green economy.

Participation in international agreements such as the Paris Agreement showcases India's efforts to balance development and environmental sustainability. India's emphasis on renewable energy and sustainable practices positions it as a key player in global climate discussions, advocating for equity and responsibility among developed and developing nations. By taking proactive measures to address climate change, India not only works towards its domestic goals but also reinforces its standing as a responsible global player.

3. Geopolitical Influence and Regional Stability

India's geopolitical significance has been magnified by its strategic location in South Asia, bordering several key nations, including China and Pakistan. The political decisions made within India have far-reaching implications for regional stability and security. India's approach to bilateral relations, particularly with its neighbors, is crucial for fostering peace and cooperation in the region.

India's participation in multilateral forums, such as the Shanghai Cooperation Organisation (SCO) and the BRICS (Brazil, Russia, India, China, and South Africa) grouping, reflects its commitment to collaborative governance and regional stability. Furthermore, India's efforts to strengthen ties with countries in the Indo-Pacific region, through initiatives like the Quad (Quadrilateral Security Dialogue) with the United States, Japan, and Australia, demonstrate its strategic intent to counterbalance China's influence while enhancing security cooperation.

4. Soft Power and Cultural Diplomacy

India's rich cultural heritage and diversity provide it with significant soft power, which plays a vital role in enhancing its global image. Through cultural diplomacy, India showcases its traditions, art, music, and cuisine, fostering goodwill and understanding among nations. Initiatives like the International Day of Yoga and the promotion of Bollywood films worldwide contribute to India's soft power narrative.

In addition to cultural exchanges, India's diaspora is a vital asset in strengthening international ties. The Indian community abroad serves as a bridge between India and other nations, promoting economic ties and cultural understanding. The government's initiatives to engage the diaspora through events and programs underscore the importance of soft power in enhancing India's global presence.

5. Challenges and Opportunities Ahead

Despite the promising prospects, India faces several challenges that could impact its global standing. Internally, issues such as political polarization, social unrest, and economic disparities can undermine the nation's cohesive approach to foreign policy. Externally, navigating complex relationships with neighboring countries and global powers, particularly in the context of trade disputes and security concerns, will require adept political maneuvering.

However, these challenges also present opportunities for India to redefine its role on the global stage. By promoting dialogue, fostering regional cooperation, and advocating for equitable policies in international forums, India can emerge as a leader in addressing global challenges.

The future of Indian politics on the global stage is a dynamic interplay of economic growth, environmental leadership, geopolitical strategies, and cultural diplomacy. As India continues to navigate the complexities of the 21st century, its political decisions will significantly shape not only its destiny but also the global order. By addressing domestic challenges, enhancing international cooperation, and promoting sustainable practices, India can solidify its position as a key player in global affairs, contributing to a more stable, equitable, and prosperous world.

Conclusion: The Future of Indian Politics

As India stands at the crossroads of unprecedented global change and domestic transformation, the trajectory of its political future holds significant implications for both its citizens and the world. The future of Indian politics will be shaped by a complex blend of old and new forces, from entrenched political traditions to rapidly emerging challenges and opportunities brought about by technology, economic reforms, and global dynamics.

A Balancing Act of Tradition and Progress

One of the key aspects that will define Indian politics moving forward is its ability to balance tradition with progress. India's political system, deeply rooted in democratic principles and a rich historical legacy, has proven resilient over decades. However, the rapidly evolving nature of society—spurred by technological advancements, increasing youth participation, and demands for social justice—requires politics to adapt. While tradition offers stability, progress offers the hope of a more inclusive, equitable, and dynamic society. Striking this balance is crucial for sustainable development.

The Role of Youth and Digital Transformation

The role of India's youth cannot be overstated in shaping the future. With over half of the population under the age of 25, the demands and aspirations of this demographic will heavily influence political priorities. As digital natives, young people will push for greater transparency, accountability, and responsiveness in government. They will also drive movements for social justice, environmental sustainability, and economic reforms, ensuring that the political system remains agile and responsive to new challenges.

Digital politics will also play a critical role in shaping the political landscape. The increasing use of technology, data analytics, and social media in elections, governance, and policy-making will redefine political engagement. However, this also brings challenges like misinformation, digital surveillance, and the potential misuse of power, which need careful regulation and ethical frameworks.

Navigating Economic Reforms and Global Challenges

India's economic policies and political decisions will have a far-reaching impact not only on its own citizens but also on its standing in the global arena. The need for robust economic reforms, particularly in addressing unemployment, infrastructure development, and fostering a business-friendly environment, is critical. Additionally, managing the delicate balance between public and private sectors, promoting innovation, and encouraging foreign investment will be vital in ensuring India's sustained economic growth.

India's role in global politics will continue to evolve, with an increasing focus on strategic partnerships, climate change leadership, and regional cooperation. As a rising global power, India must navigate the complexities of international diplomacy, security challenges, and its influence in multilateral organizations with tact and vision.

The Promise of Reform

While challenges such as corruption, political polarization, and regional disparities persist, the road ahead holds promise. Political reforms, transparency in governance, and stronger institutions can ensure that India's democratic fabric remains intact while adapting to the demands of a rapidly changing world. Grassroots movements, civil society engagement, and judicial interventions can strengthen accountability and restore trust in public institutions.

A Hopeful Future

Ultimately, the future of Indian politics rests on its ability to remain adaptable, inclusive, and forward-thinking. The engagement of citizens, the dynamism of its youth, the power of its institutions, and the spirit of reform will collectively shape the nation's political landscape. With a commitment to democratic values, transparency, and sustainable development, India has the potential to navigate its challenges and emerge as a model for governance in the 21st century.

The path forward for Indian politics is filled with opportunities for meaningful change. If pursued with integrity, innovation, and inclusiveness, the future holds immense promise for a prosperous, equitable, and influential India—one that continues to uphold its democratic ethos while embracing the possibilities of the future.

| 16 |

Final Thoughts and Call to Action

As we conclude this exploration of the intricate relationship between politics and society in India, it is essential to reflect on the crucial role that the youth must play in shaping the future of our nation. The political landscape is not static; it is dynamic, evolving, and influenced by the collective actions of informed and engaged citizens. This chapter serves as a call to action for the youth to become active participants in the political process, emphasizing the importance of being informed, engaged, and empowered to make a difference.

The Importance of Youth Participation

Youth participation is not just a desirable aspect of a vibrant democracy—it is a crucial necessity. In India, where over 50% of the population is under the age of 25, the youth hold the potential to drive transformative change in the political landscape. Their involvement is critical for ensuring that the country's policies and governance reflect the aspirations, values, and challenges of the younger generation. The importance of youth participation can be understood through several key factors:

1. Fresh Perspectives and Innovative Solutions

Young people often bring fresh, untainted perspectives to political discourse. They are less bound by the traditional, entrenched ways of thinking that have dominated the political arena for decades. This allows them to approach issues—such as unemployment, education, climate change, and social justice—with innovative ideas and a progressive mindset. By being more in tune with modern technology, global trends, and the needs of future generations, they can propose and implement solutions that address current problems more effectively.

Their participation also helps break the cycle of outdated policies and stagnant leadership that can prevent nations from evolving. The infusion of fresh ideas is essential for political systems to remain relevant and responsive to the rapidly changing world.

2. Representation of a Key Demographic

Youth represent a significant portion of the Indian electorate, yet their voices have often been underrepresented in decision-making processes. Policies directly impact their future—be it employment opportunities, educational reforms, environmental policies, or technological advancement. Ensuring their involvement in politics guarantees that their concerns, challenges, and goals are reflected in the national agenda.

As future leaders, entrepreneurs, professionals, and citizens, the policies made today will directly shape their lives tomorrow. Youth participation in politics helps ensure that decisions are not made for them without their input, but rather with their active engagement and leadership.

3. Driving Social and Political Change

Historically, young people have played an essential role in driving social and political change across the globe. From independence movements to modern-day protests for climate action, civil rights, and democracy, youth movements have been instrumental in challenging the status quo and pushing for progress. In India, too, youth activism has been at the forefront of movements like anti-corruption campaigns, gender equality advocacy, and environmental protection.

Active youth participation has the power to reshape the political discourse, bringing issues such as mental health, digital privacy, and sustainable development to the center stage. Their energy, passion, and willingness to challenge established norms make them key drivers of social transformation.

4. Engaging with Digital Politics

With the advent of digital technologies and social media, young people have a new platform for political engagement. From creating viral campaigns to mobilizing communities, digital politics allows the youth to amplify their voices and reach a broader audience. Social media platforms such as Twitter, Instagram, and YouTube have become key tools for political engagement, activism, and organizing. This is particularly relevant in a country like India, where internet penetration is rapidly increasing.

By engaging in digital politics, young people can bypass traditional barriers to political participation and directly communicate their concerns to political leaders, the media, and their peers. It is also an effective way to hold governments accountable, challenge misinformation, and promote transparency in governance.

5. Ensuring Accountability and Governance Reforms

The participation of young people is essential for fostering accountability and demanding governance reforms. They are less likely to accept corruption, nepotism, and inefficiency in politics as the norm, and more inclined to push for transparency, honesty, and merit-based systems. Their involvement challenges the complacency of established political actors and encourages reforms that can strengthen democratic institutions.

With a greater emphasis on ethics, fairness, and human rights, youth can help reimagine governance structures that are more inclusive, just, and resilient. This includes advocating for reforms such as e-governance, electoral transparency, and anti-corruption mechanisms.

6. Building a Culture of Civic Engagement

When young people participate in politics, it helps create a culture of civic engagement and responsibility. By voting, running for office, participating in debates, and engaging in activism, youth demonstrate that politics is not a distant, inaccessible field but something that everyone can—and should—be involved in. This sends a powerful message to society about the importance of participation and citizenship.

Youth participation also inspires future generations to get involved, creating a ripple effect that strengthens democratic values over time. Engaged citizens are more likely to hold their leaders accountable, vote in elections, and take active roles in their communities, contributing to a healthier and more vibrant democracy.

7. Shaping the Future

Perhaps most importantly, young people are the future leaders of the country. Their engagement today helps prepare them for the responsibilities they will take on tomorrow, be it in politics, business, social work, or any other sector. By understanding the political process, honing their leadership skills, and learning how to navigate the complexities of governance, they will be better equipped to guide the nation toward progress.

In a country as diverse and dynamic as India, the importance of youth participation cannot be overstated. The decisions made today will define the world in which they will live and lead tomorrow. Their involvement ensures that this future is shaped by a broader spectrum of ideas, experiences, and aspirations, ultimately creating a more inclusive, responsive, and innovative political system.

Call to Action

The onus is now on the youth to step up, take responsibility, and actively participate in the political process. Whether through voting, running for office, joining grassroots movements, or engaging in digital activism, there are countless ways to make a meaningful difference. India's future depends on the contributions of its young citizens, and their engagement will be key to overcoming the challenges and seizing the opportunities that lie ahead.

Activism: A Powerful Tool for Change

Activism has long been one of the most potent and transformative forces in society, driving social, political, and economic changes across the globe. In the context of Indian politics, activism has been instrumental in shaping the nation's history, from the struggle for independence to contemporary movements for justice, equality, and democracy. At its core, activism is about more than just raising awareness—it is about mobilizing people, challenging unjust systems, and pushing for meaningful reforms. In today's interconnected world, activism has become more influential than ever, empowered by digital tools and youth participation.

1. Historical Roots of Activism in India

India's political landscape has been profoundly shaped by activist movements throughout its history. The Indian independence movement, led by figures like Mahatma Gandhi, Jawaharlal Nehru, and Subhas Chandra Bose, was perhaps one of the most significant examples of political activism. Gandhi's philosophy of non-violent civil disobedience (Satyagraha) not only united millions of Indians against colonial rule but also demonstrated the power of collective action and peaceful resistance.

Post-independence, activism continued to play a critical role in addressing social and political injustices. Movements such as the Dalit movement, led by Dr. B.R. Ambedkar, sought to challenge caste-based discrimination and social inequality. The feminist movement fought for women's rights, while environmental movements, like the Chipko movement, highlighted the need for sustainable development and environmental conservation. These activist movements set the stage for modern-day activism, showing that ordinary citizens can bring about extraordinary change when united by a common cause.

2. Modern Activism: From the Streets to the Digital Sphere

In recent years, activism in India has evolved from traditional forms of protest and marches to encompass digital activism and social media campaigns. The rise of the internet and mobile technology has revolutionized the way movements are organized, communicated, and sustained. Social media platforms such as Twitter, Facebook, and Instagram have allowed activists to reach wider audiences, organize protests more efficiently, and share real-time updates on their causes.

This digital shift has also democratized activism, making it more accessible to people from all walks of life. A single hashtag can spark nationwide conversations, as seen in movements like #MeToo and #BlackLivesMatter, which have had significant impacts not only globally but also in India. Similarly, digital activism played a pivotal role in movements such as the Anti-Corruption Movement led by Anna Hazare and the nationwide protests against the Citizenship Amendment Act (CAA), where people from different backgrounds united to demand justice and accountability from the government.

The power of digital activism lies in its ability to transcend geographical and socio-economic barriers. It allows individuals to participate in meaningful political action from anywhere, whether it be by signing petitions, sharing information, or joining online discussions. Digital activism can also apply immense pressure on governments, corporations, and institutions by making public demands and drawing international attention to local issues.

3. Youth and Activism: Leading the Charge

The youth are often at the forefront of activist movements. Energized by their passion, idealism, and desire to create a better future, young people are uniquely positioned to lead social and political movements. In India, this has been demonstrated time and again. For example, during the anti-corruption protests of 2011, thousands of young people took to the streets, demanding transparency and accountability in governance. Similarly, the recent climate action protests have seen young activists like Licypriya Kangujam leading the charge for environmental justice, pushing governments to take urgent steps to combat climate change.

Youth activism is not just about making noise—it is about generating dialogue, fostering critical thinking, and pushing for concrete changes. From fighting for gender equality to advocating for sustainable development, young activists in India are addressing some of the most pressing issues of our time. Their energy, combined with the digital tools at their disposal, enables them to organize rapidly, amplify their message, and inspire others to join the cause.

4. Activism as a Catalyst for Policy Change

One of the most significant impacts of activism is its ability to influence policy decisions. Activist movements often bring issues to the forefront that political leaders or mainstream media may overlook. By creating a groundswell of public support and applying pressure through protests, petitions, and lobbying, activists can push governments to enact reforms and change policies.

For instance, the protests against the CAA and the National Register of Citizens (NRC) brought the issue of citizenship and secularism into the national spotlight, forcing the government to re-examine its stance. Similarly, the anti-corruption movement led to the passage of the Lokpal and Lokayuktas Act in 2013, which established independent anti-corruption bodies at the central and state levels. These examples illustrate that activism, when sustained and supported by the public, can lead to tangible policy changes that reshape the political landscape.

5. Challenges Faced by Activists

While activism has the potential to create significant change, it is not without its challenges. Activists often face opposition from powerful interests, including political leaders, corporations, and even law enforcement. In some cases, activists may be subject to harassment, arrest, or censorship, as seen in the crackdown on environmental and human rights activists in various parts of India. The struggle to maintain momentum and keep the public engaged over long periods can also be a challenge, especially in the face of apathy or fatigue.

Despite these challenges, activism remains a vital tool for addressing injustices and holding power accountable. The key to sustaining activism is persistence, coalition-building, and the ability to adapt to changing circumstances. Activists must also find ways to engage with a broader audience, including those who may not initially be interested in or aware of the issues at hand.

6. The Role of Media in Amplifying Activism

The media plays a crucial role in amplifying activist movements and bringing their causes to the public's attention. In the digital age, traditional media outlets, as well as independent media platforms, can shine a light on grassroots movements, ensuring that activists' voices are heard and their demands are taken seriously. Investigative journalism, in particular, has been instrumental in exposing corruption, human rights abuses, and environmental violations, often in collaboration with activist groups.

Social media, as mentioned earlier, has also given activists unprecedented power to control their narratives, bypassing traditional gatekeepers of information. However, this also means that activists need to be vigilant about the spread of misinformation and the potential for government or corporate interests to manipulate online discussions. Maintaining credibility and fostering trust with their audience is essential for the success of any activist movement.

7. The Future of Activism in India

As India continues to grapple with issues such as corruption, inequality, environmental degradation, and political polarization, activism will remain a powerful tool for change. The success of future movements will depend on their ability to mobilize citizens, sustain public interest, and push for institutional reforms. The rise of digital activism, combined with the growing engagement of young people in politics, offers a promising future for social and political change in the country.

Moreover, as India becomes increasingly interconnected with the global community, activism in India is likely to influence and be influenced by international movements for justice, equality, and sustainability. This interconnectedness creates opportunities for cross-border collaborations and solidarity, as seen in global movements for climate action, human rights, and anti-corruption.

8. Activism as a Responsibility

Finally, activism is not just a tool for those who are passionate about specific causes—it is a responsibility for all citizens in a democracy. Whether it is through voting, participating in local governance, or joining protests, every individual has a role to play in holding power accountable and ensuring that society moves toward justice, equality, and sustainability.

In India, where issues such as corruption, caste discrimination, and gender inequality persist, the need for active citizen participation is greater than ever. Activism allows ordinary citizens to challenge the status quo and demand a better future. As India continues to evolve, so too will the forms and methods of activism, but its underlying purpose will remain the same: to create a more just and equitable society for all.

Activism is a powerful force for change, capable of transforming societies, shaping policies, and inspiring future generations. In India, it has played a vital role in the nation's political and social development, and it continues to be a crucial tool for addressing the challenges of the 21st century. Whether through traditional forms of protest or digital activism, the power of collective action should not be underestimated. As young people take up the mantle of leadership, activism will remain a driving force for progress, equity, and justice.

Running for Office: A Path to Leadership

Running for office is one of the most direct and impactful ways for individuals to shape the political landscape and effect meaningful change. For those committed to public service, it represents a transition from activism or advocacy into formal leadership, allowing them to work within the system to address the challenges their communities face. In India, with its vast and diverse population, running for office comes with both immense opportunities and challenges, but it is a vital path to leadership for those looking to make a difference at the local, state, or national level.

1. The Significance of Political Participation

Political participation through running for office is crucial for a vibrant and healthy democracy. While activism can drive awareness and foster dialogue on key issues, elected officials have the power to implement policies and reforms that directly impact the lives of citizens. By stepping into public office, individuals have the chance to move from influencing political debates to actively shaping government decisions and ensuring that the voices of the people they represent are heard.

For many, running for office is about more than just seeking political power; it is about contributing to the welfare of society, promoting justice, and working toward the common good. Elected leaders can champion causes like education, healthcare, infrastructure, and social justice, translating grassroots movements into policy action. In a country like India, where the government plays a significant role in areas ranging from economic regulation to social development, holding office can be a powerful tool to drive change.

2. Challenges of Running for Office in India

Despite its potential, running for office in India is not without its hurdles. The political landscape can be highly competitive and, at times, fraught with issues such as corruption, nepotism, and entrenched party structures. For newcomers or independents, the journey can be particularly daunting. Running against well-established political figures or entrenched party systems can be challenging, especially in constituencies where money and political influence dominate.

Additionally, elections in India often come with financial and logistical challenges. Campaigning can be expensive, and candidates without access to significant financial resources may find it difficult to compete. This has historically limited the participation of people from marginalized or economically disadvantaged backgrounds. However, recent reforms, such as the introduction of transparency laws and stricter regulations on campaign finance, are aimed at leveling the playing field.

The electoral process itself, with its lengthy timelines and bureaucratic hurdles, can also be a challenge. Candidates must navigate a complex system of nomination, campaigning, and compliance with the Election Commission's rules, all while maintaining a connection with the electorate. These hurdles, though significant, should not dissuade aspiring leaders, as overcoming them is a necessary step in becoming a true representative of the people.

3. The Role of Youth in Politics

In recent years, there has been a growing recognition of the importance of youth participation in politics. Young people are not just the future leaders of tomorrow; they are essential to shaping the present. Youth candidates bring fresh perspectives, energy, and innovative ideas to the political arena, challenging the status quo and addressing issues that may be overlooked by older generations.

In India, where a significant portion of the population is under the age of 35, the representation of young people in politics is crucial for addressing the needs and aspirations of this demographic. From unemployment to education reform, healthcare to climate action, young candidates are often more attuned to the issues that affect their peers and are more likely to champion progressive policies that address these challenges.

Young leaders like Hardik Patel and Kanhaiya Kumar have already made significant impacts in Indian politics, demonstrating that youth candidates can rally large followings and influence national debates. They serve as inspirations for the next generation of political leaders who want to challenge the established order and advocate for the rights and welfare of the youth and marginalized communities.

4. Steps to Running for Office

For those who wish to take the step from advocacy to candidacy, understanding the process of running for office is essential. The first step is identifying the level of government where one wishes to serve, whether it be local municipalities, state assemblies, or national parliament. Each level of government presents different challenges and opportunities, and candidates must be clear about where they can make the most impact based on their expertise and understanding of local issues.

Once a decision is made, prospective candidates must align themselves with a political party or choose to run as an independent. Aligning with a party can offer significant support in terms of resources, recognition, and established voter bases. However, running as an independent can provide greater freedom to advocate for specific issues without adhering to a party's agenda.

Building a strong campaign is the next critical step. This includes forming a campaign team, developing a clear and compelling message, and connecting with voters on the ground. In India, grassroots campaigning—meeting people in their homes, listening to their concerns, and earning their trust—remains one of the most effective ways to win elections, particularly in local and rural constituencies.

Candidates must also be prepared to deal with the media, both traditional and digital. Having a clear communication strategy, engaging with journalists, and using social media platforms effectively can help candidates reach a wider audience and build their reputation.

5. Why Running for Office Matters

Running for office is not just about personal ambition—it is about representation and ensuring that the voices of all citizens are heard in the halls of power. In a diverse democracy like India, it is vital that leaders come from different backgrounds, castes, religions, and genders to reflect the nation's varied population. More representation in government leads to more inclusive policy-making, addressing the needs of every section of society.

By choosing to run for office, individuals take on the responsibility of not just representing their constituents but also of upholding democratic values. They become part of the checks and balances that ensure accountability in governance. Elected officials have the power to challenge injustices, reform outdated systems, and advocate for policies that promote equality, justice, and progress. Through their leadership, they can create a ripple effect, inspiring others in their communities to become more engaged in the political process.

6. Inspiring a New Generation of Leaders

For a country to thrive, it must continuously cultivate new leaders who are committed to public service and the well-being of society. Running for office is a way to inspire others, particularly young people, to take an active role in politics. Those who step up as candidates set an example for others, showing that political engagement is not the domain of a select few but is open to anyone willing to serve the public.

Programs such as the National Youth Parliament Festival and the participation of young leaders in organizations like the Indian Youth Congress or the Akhil Bharatiya Vidyarthi Parishad (ABVP) demonstrate that there are pathways for young people to enter politics and make a real difference. As more young leaders enter the political arena, they will bring with them new ideas, modern approaches, and a willingness to challenge the status quo.

7. The Future of Indian Leadership

The future of leadership in India will be shaped by those who are willing to step forward, run for office, and serve their communities. As politics becomes more inclusive and diverse, the hope is that new leaders will address the deep-rooted issues that have long affected India, from poverty and inequality to corruption and environmental degradation.

Ultimately, running for office is a powerful way to lead by example. It requires courage, commitment, and a genuine desire to make a positive difference. By taking this step, individuals can help build a more just, equitable, and democratic India, where the voices of all citizens are heard and respected.

Running for office is a path to leadership that offers individuals the opportunity to serve their communities and bring about real, lasting change. Despite the challenges, it is a rewarding journey that allows candidates to contribute to the betterment of society and to be part of the decision-making process that shapes the future of the country. As India's political landscape continues to evolve, the participation of new leaders—especially young, diverse, and passionate individuals—will be key to ensuring that the nation remains vibrant, democratic, and forward-looking.

Conclusion: A Call to Action

The conclusion of Chapter 15 serves as a rallying cry, a call to action that emphasizes the responsibility of every individual, especially the youth, in shaping the future of Indian politics. At its core, it conveys that democracy is not a spectator sport—it requires active participation, engagement, and dedication from all citizens to ensure its vitality and success. In an age where challenges are growing more complex, from economic disparities to social injustices, the need for proactive involvement in the political process is greater than ever.

1. The Power of Individual Action

At the heart of democracy lies the power of the individual—the belief that every voice matters and that every person has the potential to contribute to societal progress. This conclusion stresses that change doesn't solely rest in the hands of elected officials but begins with each citizen taking responsibility for their community and country. Whether through voting, activism, running for office, or participating in civic initiatives, individuals can make a tangible difference.

The youth, in particular, must recognize the unique position they hold as catalysts for change. They are not just the leaders of tomorrow, but the leaders of today, with the energy, passion, and creativity needed to address the pressing issues facing the nation. By harnessing their potential and stepping into roles of leadership, young people can drive forward meaningful reforms and innovations that will define India's future.

2. Active Citizenship: More Than Just Voting

While voting is one of the most powerful tools in a democracy, this conclusion emphasizes that being an active citizen goes beyond just casting a ballot. It involves staying informed about political issues, holding elected officials accountable, and advocating for policies that align with the values of justice, equality, and fairness. It also involves taking an interest in local governance and community issues, understanding that change often begins at the grassroots level.

Citizens can also participate by volunteering with political or social organizations, contributing to discussions on public policy, and supporting causes that promote the public good. By engaging in civic life and encouraging others to do the same, individuals can help create a more inclusive and participatory democracy.

3. The Importance of Collective Effort

The conclusion underscores the need for collective effort in the fight against the political and social challenges facing India. Corruption, inequality, and polarization are not issues that can be solved by individuals alone. They require the collaboration of communities, civil society, government institutions, and the private sector. Each of these actors plays a critical role in fostering a political environment that is accountable, transparent, and oriented toward the welfare of all citizens.

Youth movements, grassroots campaigns, and civil society organizations can act as powerful vehicles for collective action. By coming together, people can amplify their voices and push for reforms that address systemic problems, whether in education, healthcare, employment, or governance.

4. Building a More Just and Inclusive Society

The conclusion calls for the construction of a more just and inclusive society—one where every citizen, regardless of background, has the opportunity to thrive. This vision cannot be realized unless the root causes of inequality, discrimination, and disenfranchisement are tackled head-on. Political participation, especially by historically marginalized groups such as women, minorities, and economically disadvantaged individuals, is essential to achieving this goal.

It is through political engagement and leadership that these groups can challenge the status quo, advocate for their rights, and bring about transformative change. By encouraging a more diverse range of candidates to run for office and by promoting policies that address the needs of all citizens, India can build a democracy that truly reflects its rich diversity.

5. A Vision for the Future: Hope and Action

Ultimately, this conclusion is about hope—hope that through collective action, young leadership, and active participation, the future of Indian politics can be brighter and more inclusive. It acknowledges that the road ahead may be difficult, but it also insists that the challenges can be overcome with commitment and perseverance.

This chapter ends with a call to every reader to take ownership of their role in democracy. Whether through small acts of civic engagement or large-scale leadership efforts, each person has the ability to contribute to a more just and equitable society. The future of Indian politics is not something that will be handed down by a few; it will be shaped by the many—by citizens who care enough to act.

6. The Legacy of Today's Actions

The conclusion also reminds readers that the actions taken today will shape the legacy of tomorrow. The political landscape that future generations inherit will be the product of the decisions and efforts made now. Therefore, it is incumbent upon the youth, activists, politicians, and everyday citizens to ensure that they leave behind a political system that is more democratic, more just, and more responsive to the needs of all its people.

By answering this call to action, individuals can help lay the foundation for a future where political participation is widespread, corruption is minimized, and the government is a true reflection of the will of the people.

Final Thoughts

In closing, this chapter offers a powerful and optimistic vision for the future of Indian politics, one that is driven by the energy, participation, and leadership of its citizens, especially the youth. It challenges readers to not only imagine a better future but to take the steps necessary to achieve it. Through active citizenship, engagement, and collective effort, the chapter urges everyone to become part of the change they wish to see, reinforcing the idea that a truly democratic and just India is within reach—if only we are willing to work for it.

Appendix

Key Terms and Political Jargon Explained in Simple Language

The world of politics can often seem daunting due to the complex terminology and jargon that are commonly used. This appendix aims to break down key political terms and concepts into simple, accessible language, making it easier for readers to understand the foundational ideas behind political discourse. Whether you're new to politics or seeking to clarify certain terms, this section will serve as a handy reference.

1. Democracy

Definition: A form of government where power is vested in the hands of the people, either directly or through elected representatives.

Explanation: In a democracy, citizens have the right to vote and participate in decision-making processes. The government is accountable to the people and must govern according to laws and regulations that protect individual freedoms and rights.

2. Republic

Definition: A type of democracy where the head of state is an elected or nominated president rather than a monarch.

Explanation: In a republic like India, the people elect representatives to govern on their behalf, and the president is the symbolic leader of the country, distinct from the elected parliament.

3. Federalism

Definition: A system of government where power is divided between a central (national) government and individual state governments.

Explanation: India is a federal country, meaning the central government in New Delhi shares power with state governments. Each state has the ability to make decisions on certain issues, while other matters are handled by the central government.

4. Constitution

Definition: The fundamental law of a country that outlines how the government works, including the rights and responsibilities of citizens and government bodies.

Explanation: The Constitution of India is the supreme law of the land. It defines how the government functions, the division of powers, and the fundamental rights that all citizens are entitled to.

5. Legislature

Definition: The branch of government responsible for making laws.

Explanation: In India, the legislature consists of the Parliament at the national level and the Legislative Assemblies at the state level. These bodies create laws, approve budgets, and hold the government accountable.

6. Executive

Definition: The branch of government responsible for implementing and enforcing laws.

Explanation: The executive in India includes the Prime Minister, the Cabinet, and other governmental agencies. They are responsible for day-to-day administration and governance.

7. Judiciary

Definition: The system of courts that interprets and applies the law in the name of the state.

Explanation: The judiciary in India ensures that laws are followed and protects the rights of individuals. It can declare laws or actions of the government unconstitutional if they violate the principles of justice.

8. Political Party

Definition: An organized group of people with shared political views that seeks to gain political power by winning elections.

Explanation: Political parties in India, such as the Bharatiya Janata Party (BJP) or the Indian National Congress (INC), represent different ideologies and work to implement their policies by contesting elections.

9. Ideology

Definition: A set of beliefs, values, and principles that guide the political goals and actions of an individual, group, or political party.

Explanation: Political ideologies such as socialism, capitalism, and liberalism influence how governments make decisions and how parties shape their manifestos.

10. Secularism

Definition: The principle of separating religion from government and ensuring equal treatment of all religions by the state.

Explanation: In India, secularism means that the government does not favor any religion and treats all citizens equally, regardless of their religious beliefs.

11. Coalition

Definition: An alliance of different political parties that come together to form a government, usually because no single party has won a majority in elections.

Explanation: Coalition governments are common in India's multi-party system. When one party doesn't have enough seats to form a government, it partners with others to create a majority in the legislature.

12. Election

Definition: The process by which citizens vote to choose their representatives in government.

Explanation: Elections in India are held at various levels—local, state, and national. The process is overseen by the Election Commission of India, which ensures that elections are free and fair.

13. First-Past-the-Post (FPTP)

Definition: An electoral system in which the candidate with the most votes wins, even if they do not get more than half of the votes.

Explanation: In India, elections for both the Lok Sabha (House of the People) and state legislatures use the FPTP system, where candidates in each constituency compete, and the one with the highest number of votes wins.

14. Lok Sabha

Definition: The lower house of India's Parliament, consisting of members directly elected by the people.

Explanation: The Lok Sabha is the house where laws are proposed, debated, and passed. It plays a key role in forming the government, as the party with the most members in the Lok Sabha usually forms the ruling government.

15. Rajya Sabha

Definition: The upper house of India's Parliament, with members who are either elected by state legislatures or appointed by the president.

Explanation: The Rajya Sabha represents the states of India and provides a check on the Lok Sabha. It reviews and suggests changes to legislation passed by the lower house.

16. Electoral Constituency

Definition: A geographic area represented by an elected official in the legislature.

Explanation: India is divided into constituencies for elections to the Lok Sabha and state assemblies. Each constituency elects one representative to the relevant legislative body.

17. Opposition

Definition: The political parties or groups that are not part of the ruling government and provide an alternative viewpoint in the legislature.

Explanation: The opposition plays a critical role in holding the government accountable and ensuring that all policies and actions are in the best interest of the public.

18. Manifesto

Definition: A document released by a political party before an election, outlining its policies and plans if it is elected to power.

Explanation: Political parties in India release manifestos during election campaigns, detailing their stance on various issues such as economy, education, and healthcare.

19. Bureaucracy

Definition: The system of government officials and agencies that implement laws and policies.

Explanation: Bureaucrats are the civil servants who work behind the scenes in various government departments, ensuring the smooth operation of government services and the implementation of policies.

20. Populism

Definition: A political approach that seeks to represent the interests of ordinary people, often by making large-scale promises or focusing on grievances against the elite.

Explanation: Populist leaders appeal to the masses by promising quick solutions to complex problems, often through emotional rhetoric, sometimes bypassing rational policymaking.

21. Public Sector

Definition: The part of the economy that is controlled by the government, including services like education, healthcare, and transportation.

Explanation: Public sector jobs are those within government agencies or state-owned enterprises. In India, companies like Indian Railways and Bharat Heavy Electricals Limited (BHEL) are public sector enterprises.

22. Private Sector

Definition: The part of the economy that is owned and operated by private individuals or companies, not the government.

Explanation: Companies like Tata, Reliance, and Infosys operate in the private sector, contributing significantly to India's economy through innovation, job creation, and economic development.

23. Corruption

Definition: The misuse of power or position for personal gain.

Explanation: Corruption can occur at any level of government, from bureaucrats accepting bribes to politicians engaging in unethical behavior. It is a major challenge to governance in India.

24. Lobbying

Definition: The act of attempting to influence the decisions of government officials, often by special interest groups or corporations.

Explanation: Lobbying is a common practice where individuals or organizations try to persuade lawmakers to pass legislation that benefits their cause or business.

25. Judicial Review

Definition: The power of the judiciary to review laws or government actions and declare them unconstitutional if they violate the Constitution.

Explanation: In India, the Supreme Court and High Courts have the power of judicial review to ensure that the government does not overstep its authority or infringe upon citizens' rights.

Understanding these key terms is essential for engaging with political discussions and processes, especially in a democracy like India. These simplified definitions should provide clarity and help demystify some of the jargon used in political debates, making the subject more accessible to everyone. The appendix serves as a guide to navigating the often complex world of politics, encouraging informed and active participation.

Key Laws

Summary of Key Laws and Reforms Mentioned in the Book

Throughout the book, several significant laws and reforms have been discussed, reflecting the evolving political, social, and economic landscape of India. These key legislative measures have been instrumental in shaping the nation's governance, democracy, economy, and welfare systems. Below is a detailed summary of the most important laws and reforms mentioned in the book:

1. The Constitution of India (1950)

The Indian Constitution, adopted in 1950, is the supreme law of the land, providing the framework for political governance and social justice. It enshrines fundamental rights, duties, and the principles of equality, liberty, and fraternity. The Constitution also establishes the structure of government at the central and state levels, guaranteeing a federal system of governance with a parliamentary democracy.

- **Key Features**: Fundamental Rights (Article 12-35), Directive Principles of State Policy (Article 36-51), and the structure of the Executive, Legislature, and Judiciary.

2. The Representation of the People Act (1951)

This law is essential for the conduct of elections to Parliament and state legislatures. It provides for the qualifications and disqualifications for membership, the process of elections, and the management of election-related offenses.

- **Key Features**: Regulation of election expenses, guidelines for political campaigns, and the conduct of free and fair elections.

3. Anti-Corruption Laws

a) The Prevention of Corruption Act (1988) The Prevention of Corruption Act is a critical law aimed at curbing corruption among public servants. It criminalizes the act of accepting or offering bribes, misusing power, and corrupt practices within government offices. The Act has been amended over the years to strengthen the fight against corruption.

- **Key Features**: Definitions of public servants, bribes, and criminal misconduct, along with the legal process for investigation and prosecution.

b) The Lokpal and Lokayuktas Act (2013) This law established independent anti-corruption bodies—Lokpal at the central level and Lokayuktas at the state level—to investigate allegations of corruption against public officials, including the Prime Minister, ministers, and members of Parliament.

- **Key Features**: Empowerment of Lokpal and Lokayuktas to investigate corruption cases, provision for a special court to prosecute corruption cases.

4. Right to Information (RTI) Act (2005)

The RTI Act is a landmark law that empowers Indian citizens to seek information from public authorities, promoting transparency and accountability in government operations.

- **Key Features**: Citizens can request information from any public authority; mandatory disclosure of information by public authorities to foster transparency.

5. Goods and Services Tax (GST) Act (2017)

The GST Act introduced a unified tax system, replacing multiple indirect taxes levied by the central and state governments. The GST is a comprehensive, destination-based tax applied on goods and services at a national level.

- **Key Features**: Simplified tax structure, removal of tax barriers between states, and promotion of a unified market for goods and services.

6. The National Rural Employment Guarantee Act (NREGA) (2005)

Also known as the Mahatma Gandhi National Rural Employment Guarantee Act (MGNREGA), this law provides a legal guarantee for at least 100 days of wage employment in rural areas to enhance livelihood security. It aims to improve the purchasing power of the rural population, particularly unskilled workers.

- **Key Features**: Guaranteed employment, focus on rural development, and empowerment of local governance (Panchayati Raj).

7. The Land Acquisition, Rehabilitation, and Resettlement Act (2013)

This law was introduced to ensure fair compensation and rehabilitation for those affected by land acquisition for industrialization, infrastructure, and urbanization. It replaced the colonial-era Land Acquisition Act of 1894.

- **Key Features**: Provision for fair compensation, rehabilitation and resettlement of displaced families, and environmental safeguards.

8. Demonetization (2016)

Demonetization refers to the government's decision to invalidate high-denomination currency notes (₹500 and ₹1,000) in 2016. The move was aimed at curbing black money, counterfeiting, and corruption. While not a law, demonetization had a profound impact on the Indian economy.

- **Key Features**: Elimination of specific currency notes, promotion of digital payments, and tightening of the informal economy.

9. The Farm Laws (2020) [Now Repealed]

The three controversial farm laws—*The Farmers' Produce Trade and Commerce Act, The Farmers Agreement on Price Assurance and Farm Services Act*, and *The Essential Commodities Act (Amendment)*—were introduced to reform the agricultural sector by deregulating markets and promoting contract farming. After widespread protests from farmers, these laws were repealed in 2021.

- **Key Features**: Promotion of private markets outside state-regulated APMCs, contractual agreements between farmers and buyers, and loosening of stockpiling restrictions on certain essential commodities.

10. Education Policies and Reforms

a) The Right of Children to Free and Compulsory Education (RTE) Act (2009) This law guarantees free and compulsory education to children aged 6-14 years. It places the onus on the state to ensure the provision of adequate schooling facilities and infrastructure.

- **Key Features**: Free elementary education, minimum infrastructure standards, and provisions for disadvantaged children.

b) National Education Policy (NEP) (2020) The NEP 2020 introduced sweeping reforms in the education sector, aiming to make education more inclusive, multidisciplinary, and future-oriented. It focuses on developing critical thinking, vocational skills, and holistic learning.

- **Key Features**: Flexible curriculum, focus on early childhood education, integration of technology, and emphasis on regional languages.

11. Welfare Schemes

a) The Public Distribution System (PDS) The PDS is a nation-wide food security system that provides subsidized food grains to the poor. It is a crucial tool in addressing hunger and poverty in India.

- **Key Features**: Distribution of essential commodities like wheat, rice, and sugar at subsidized rates through fair-price shops.

b) Pradhan Mantri Jan Dhan Yojana (PMJDY) Launched in 2014, PMJDY is a financial inclusion program aimed at ensuring access to financial services such as bank accounts, remittances, credit, and insurance for all citizens, especially the underprivileged.

- **Key Features**: Zero-balance bank accounts, direct benefit transfer, and financial literacy programs.

12. Electoral Reforms

a) Voter Verifiable Paper Audit Trail (VVPAT) Introduced as part of electoral reforms, VVPAT is a method that allows voters to verify their vote through a printed paper receipt after voting in an Electronic Voting Machine (EVM).

- **Key Features**: Enhances transparency in voting, ensures the integrity of elections, and increases voter confidence.

The above-mentioned laws, reforms, and policies have significantly influenced India's political, social, and economic trajectory. They address critical issues ranging from corruption and electoral integrity to economic liberalization, education, and welfare. These reforms represent India's ongoing efforts to modernize its legal and governance systems while addressing the aspirations and needs of its diverse population. By understanding these key laws and reforms, readers can better appreciate the complexities of Indian governance and the continuous evolution of its democracy.

References

List of Resources for Further Reading

To deepen your understanding of the complex political, economic, and social issues discussed throughout the book, this section provides a list of carefully selected resources. These include books, articles, websites, and academic journals that offer additional perspectives, historical context, and in-depth analyses. By exploring these materials, readers can further enrich their knowledge and engage more critically with contemporary political discourse.

1. Books

a) ***India After Gandhi: The History of the World's Largest Democracy*** **by Ramachandra Guha** One of the most comprehensive books on modern Indian history, Guha's work offers a detailed account of post-independence India. It examines the political challenges, social changes, and economic evolution that have shaped the country since 1947.

b) ***The Idea of India*** **by Sunil Khilnani** This influential book explores India's political identity and national consciousness. Khilnani reflects on the challenges of democracy, secularism, and nation-building in a diverse country like India.

c) ***An Uncertain Glory: India and its Contradictions*** **by Jean Drèze and Amartya Sen** This critical examination of India's development highlights the economic disparities and social challenges that persist despite rapid growth. Drèze and Sen delve into the importance of public services, inequality, and the role of the state in development.

d) ***The Argumentative Indian: Writings on Indian History, Culture and Identity*** **by Amartya Sen** Amartya Sen offers a unique perspective on India's intellectual traditions, social history, and the importance of public debate. This collection of essays is crucial for anyone interested in understanding the democratic and pluralistic ethos of India.

e) *The Gita for a Global World: Ethical Action in an Age of Flux* **by Rohit Chopra**

A contemporary interpretation of the Bhagavad Gita, this book connects ancient Indian philosophy with modern-day ethical and political challenges. It offers insight into the relevance of ancient texts in addressing current global issues.

f) *The Globalization of World Politics: An Introduction to International Relations* **by John Baylis, Steve Smith, and Patricia Owens**

For those interested in the global context of Indian politics, this book provides a thorough introduction to international relations and globalization. It covers important themes like global governance, security, and the politics of development.

2. Articles and Reports

a) *Democracy in India: Successes, Failures, and the Future* **by Milan Vaishnav (Carnegie Endowment for International Peace)** This article explores the state of democracy in India, focusing on its achievements and ongoing challenges. Vaishnav discusses issues like political corruption, the rise of populism, and electoral politics.

b) *The Rise of Political Polarization in India* **by Neelanjan Sircar (Brookings Institution)** Sircar offers a comprehensive analysis of the growing political polarization in India. The article explains how caste, religion, and regional identity play a role in shaping the political landscape.

c) *Decoding India's Economic Reforms* **by Arvind Panagariya (Columbia University Press)** This report provides an in-depth look at India's economic reforms since the 1990s, explaining how liberalization has impacted various sectors of the economy, from agriculture to technology.

d) *The Role of Media in Indian Politics* **by Sevanti Ninan (Economic and Political Weekly)** Ninan explores how Indian media has shaped and been shaped by political forces. She provides an insightful analysis of media's role in elections, public opinion, and political narratives.

3. Websites and Online Resources

a) PRS Legislative Research (prsindia.org) This non-profit organization provides detailed analysis of legislation and policy in India. The site is a valuable resource for understanding parliamentary procedures, recent bills, and government policies.

b) Election Commission of India (eci.gov.in) For anyone interested in India's electoral process, the official website of the Election Commission offers comprehensive data on elections, voter registration, and election results.

c) IndiaStat (indiastat.com) IndiaStat is a statistical database that provides access to a wealth of information on India's economy, demographics, education, and development indicators. It is useful for those seeking data-driven insights into policy and political issues.

d) Centre for the Study of Developing Societies (csds.in) CSDS conducts extensive research on political behavior, electoral trends, and democracy in India. Their reports and surveys offer critical insights into public opinion and voter behavior.

4. Academic Journals

a) Economic and Political Weekly (EPW) One of India's most respected academic journals, EPW covers a wide range of topics including politics, economics, social justice, and international relations. It is a must-read for those interested in serious academic discussions about India's political and economic landscape.

b) The Indian Journal of Political Science (IJPS) IJPS is a peer-reviewed journal that publishes articles on political theory, public policy, and governance in India. It is an excellent resource for students and researchers.

c) Journal of Democracy This international journal provides insights into global democracy, including detailed analysis of India's democratic journey. It frequently features articles on the challenges and successes of democracy in developing nations.

d) Asian Survey A quarterly journal that focuses on the politics and economics of Asia, *Asian Survey* often includes scholarly articles on India's foreign policy, regional power dynamics, and economic reforms.

5. Documentaries and Videos

a) India's Road to Independence (BBC Documentary) This documentary chronicles India's struggle for independence and the early years of nation-building. It offers historical context and insight into the challenges faced by India's first leaders.

b) Inside India's COVID Crisis (PBS Frontline) A powerful documentary on how India grappled with the COVID-19 pandemic, offering an analysis of the government's response, public health infrastructure, and the socio-economic impact.

c) India's Rising: The Politics of Change (Al Jazeera) This documentary examines India's changing political landscape, focusing on issues like economic reforms, political polarization, and grassroots movements.

These resources serve as a starting point for those who wish to explore the complex, multifaceted nature of Indian politics and its impact on society and the economy. By engaging with these books, articles, and academic journals, readers can deepen their understanding of the political forces that shape India's present and future. Whether you're a student, researcher, or a curious reader, these materials will provide you with valuable insights into the dynamic world of Indian politics and governance.

Author's Message

Author's Message

Dear Readers,

In today's fast-paced world, politics touches every aspect of our lives. As citizens, especially as young people, educators, and mentors, it's crucial that we understand the power of informed participation. Through Politics 101, I aim to equip you with the knowledge needed to navigate the political landscape, not just as observers but as active contributors to the future of our nation.

To the youth, you are the future. Your voice and actions matter more than ever. I urge you to engage deeply, question the status quo, and drive the changes you wish to see. Politics isn't just about elections; it's about shaping the society you live in every day.

To teachers and educators, you have the immense responsibility of guiding young minds. By instilling critical thinking and awareness about politics, you empower the next generation to be responsible, informed citizens who can actively participate in democracy.

Together, we can create a future where politics serves people, fosters development, and upholds justice. Let this book be the first step in understanding that power lies in knowledge, action, and unity.

Warm regards,

Er Sandeep Chavan

About Author

About the Author

Er Sandeep Chavan is a mechanical engineer turned educator with over 22 years of experience in the fields of industry and education. Passionate about empowering young minds, he has dedicated his career to teaching Physics, Chemistry, and Mathematics to high school students, while also nurturing their understanding of the socio-political landscape.

With a deep commitment to fostering informed citizenship, Sandeep brings a unique perspective to the realm of politics, combining his engineering background with a focus on critical thinking and practical understanding. As a writer and educator, he seeks to demystify complex political concepts and inspire the next generation to actively participate in democracy.

In Politics 101, Sandeep Chavan aims to unlock the secrets of power and corruption, offering readers a comprehensive overview of Indian politics that is both accessible and engaging. Join him on this journey to discover how informed citizens can shape the future of their nation.